Get the Edge at
Blackjack

A Scoblete Get-the-Edge Guide

Get the Edge at Blackjack

Revolutionary Advantage-Play Methods That Work!

by John May

Foreword by Frank Scoblete

Bonus Books, Inc.
Chicago, Illinois

04 03 02 01 00   5 4 3 2 1

Library of Congress Control Number: 00-109844
ISBN: 1-56625-151-6

Bonus Books, Inc.
160 East Illinois Street
Chicago, Illinois 60611

Printed in the United States of America

Merche—aun pienzo en ti durante las horas del crepulsco

Table of Contents

Part III: The Future and the Fine Points of Professional Play

Appendices

Foreword

by Frank Scoblete

The book you are holding is a blackjack nuclear bomb. There is information in it that has never before appeared in print in a mainstream book and there is some information that has never appeared anywhere except in the secret world inhabited by a handful of elite professional blackjack players. I'm sure you've seen the advertisements that say: "Learn what the casinos don't want you to know!" Often such hype is just a phony come-on for a worthless get-rich-quick system that the casinos would love for you to employ in their environs. Well, now you are going to get the chance to learn *real* strategies that not only the casinos don't want you to know, but that many of the greatest blackjack players would prefer to keep all to themselves. They are known as advantage-play methods because they give the player the advantage over the casino. They range from the widely-known though sadly little-practiced method of card counting all the way to devastating methods designed to ascertain the rank of the *very next card* coming out of the deck or shoe! Author John May has taken actual blackjack advantage play *in the casinos*—as opposed to mere theorizing in books and papers—to new levels of sophistication, daring and power, and he is going to share his thoughts, strategies and secrets with you in this volume.

Some of you reading this introduction already know who John May is. Those of you who subscribe to my magazine *The New Chance and Circumstance* or visit my website on RGT online (www.scoblete.com) have read many of his articles. John also has a large following on his own website known as The Card Counter's Cafe. If you have never made John May's acquaintance, let me make the introductions.

John May is an advantage player with an attitude. He is the author of the ineptly titled but brilliant *Baccarat for the Clueless* published by the defunct Carol Publishing Group. He's a gambling gunslinger who makes his living shooting the casinos right in the heart of their treasuries. In truth, it would not be a stretch to say that he is one of a small handful of professional players who can beat the casinos out of large sums of money on a regular basis and does just that. Unlike most gaming authors who make their living either writing about gaming or doing something else, May makes his living hammering the casinos. He writes about his techniques and shares his strategies because he's passionate about his chosen profession. I first wrote about him in my *Baccarat Battle Book* where I did an extensive interview with him concerning his advantage-play techniques in baccarat.

When Bonus Books and I decided to create the "Scoblete Get-the-Edge Guides," his name came immediately to mind. I thought, "Wouldn't it be great to get the most daring blackjack player on the planet to pen an advantage-play book that boldly goes where. . ."—well, you get the picture. So did he, and so this book.

Certainly, he shows you the ins and outs of card counting, as do many good, popular books. But May also shows us methods for beating supposedly unbeatable games, games that card counters would avoid like the plague! Ever hear of card steering? Card sequencing? Shadow play? Here's one that will blow your mind—the *stacker* play! All these—*and more*—John May has done successfully in casinos, under real-world conditions, in order to put bread on his table—lots and lots of bread. And how about beating those shuffle machines that are seemingly unbeatable by ordinary advantage players? May shows you how to beat them, too! Finally, May tackles the newest frontier of casino play—the Internet—and shows how to turn a profit there as well.

Those in the know are in awe of John May's blackjack knowledge. To say that I am proud to have him writing one of the first books of my "Scoblete Get-the-Edge Guides" is an understatement. When you read this book from cover to cover, you'll understand why I wanted him with me on this project, and you'll also see why the casino earth trembles and the casino executives cower when they hear that John May is in town. If you successfully learn and put into effect even 20 percent of what May writes about in this book, there will be lots and lots of bread on your table too—and in your pockets and bank account as well!

Part 1
Basic Strategy and Card Counting

The Fundamentals of Winning Play

Chapter 1

Blackjack Is the New Rock 'n' Roll

More people go to casinos than go to all the rap, rock, hip hop, pop, jazz, and classical music concerts combined. Most of these people pay a heavy price for their casino pleasures, a price far steeper than a concert ticket. But you can be a cultural icon, a statistical rebel, and arm yourself with a system that will shear that golden multi-million dollar casino fleece! You don't have to be a famous recording star to sing on the casino gambling stage; you just have to place your bets—and win them! And I'll show you how.

This book contains the key to winning at the only generally acknowledged casino gambling game that can be beaten legally—blackjack.

There are more myths, generalizations, and inaccuracies perpetrated by authors concerning this game than any other game in the casino. Moreover many blackjack books often contain erroneous or unhelpful information. You do not need any qualifications or credentials to write a book on blackjack. Indeed, the most successful books are often those that tell gamblers what they want to hear rather than what is correct.

This is a pity because, despite all the pitfalls that exist in blackjack, the player does stand a fighting chance against the casino when adequately informed and in possession of a proper playing system. There is money to be made on that green and pleasant baize. If you study this book *thoroughly and train yourself to play perfectly* you will be among a handful of elite individuals who can bend the laws of chance to their advantage: you'll be a card counter. What's more, you'll also be armed with advantage-play techniques that few card counters possess—techniques that many casinos have no idea exist!

It is not nearly as hard to play expert blackjack as you might think. It takes an average of five hours to learn how to play your hands and master the simplest counting system, the Ace-five. This will give you a small advantage over the house. To play blackjack professionally requires several months of study. But this is relatively little time when compared to the effort necessary to become competent in law, medicine or even some other game such as chess. Moreover, there are secrets in this book that very few experts are aware of. Much of the advanced methods described later in this book have never been published before and for a very good reason. They show clearly how it is still possible, despite all the countermeasures and game protection, to get rich, *albeit slowly*, at the blackjack tables.

The Score

The casino is noisy and crowded, it contains the perfect conditions to become invisible. In any case I have cultivated the persona of an affluent loser, having played an initial cover session here yesterday. I stroll to the bar and make small talk with the pretty bartender. She asks me what I do and I tell her I'm researching a book on gambling. Always steer as close to the truth as possible, never tell a lie, just be economical with the facts. That is my motto.

I wander upstairs with a drink. I amble over to the roulette table and buy a stack of chips. Their collective value is very little, about $60, but the sheer physical space they occupy looks impressive. I bet wildly and once spill the chips all over the baize. The chips are soon all back with the dealer.

Then several spaces open at a blackjack table, just within my peripheral field of vision. I move haphazardly over and count down the cards as they are dealt. This is a terrible game, six decks with two decks cut out of play. Most card counters would avoid it like the plague. But I am not most card counters. The Aces and 10s splash the felt and I make several winning plays, culminating in a lucrative double-down. I've won too much too fast, though there is no heat . . . yet. I pick up my chips, this is a most desirable time to quit. Chance has been kind to me because I have given her the best possible reason to do so—I always take my best shot when I have the edge! In the duel with "fate" I have the superior weaponry.

This duel of the fates continually repeats itself in the twilight hours, across the felt face of the whole casino world, with the casinos heavy favorites to win over the players. Not so with me. I am the favorite.

Many people ask: "How can you, one lone person, possibly win consistently against a massive industry with a take in the billions?" In truth, I do not go against the casinos alone. I have the accumulated wisdom of the ages and allies such as Cardano, Pascal, Epstein, and Thorp. I have the disciplines of statistics, probability, and psychology in my corner. The casinos have business school graduates or former dealers on their side. They don't stand a chance against me!

Grand are the foundations of the palaces of fortune; huge are the the pillars that support Las Vegas, Atlantic City, Monte Carlo and Mayfair. Long are their histories. But I have my own predecessors, a rich and resonant heritage as rich and resourceful as that of the casinos themselves and much, much more cunning than the casinos can ever hope to be.

The Rules of Blackjack

Blackjack is an adversarial contest between the player and the dealer. Up to seven players may compete at any time. The dealer plays for the house (the casino) and plays by lockstep house rules. The player first makes a bet, which must fall between the minimum and maximum stakes of the table; typically a table minimum will be from $5 to $50, a table maximum from $1,000 to $5,000 or even more. The dealer then deals two cards to each player and one face-up to himself. The object of the game is to beat the dealer. This can be done in two ways. One is to obtain a total which is greater than the dealer's but is not greater than 21; the other is to have the dealer bust by going over 21 while the player has a hand that is 21 or less. An Ace counts as 1 or 11 (if this does not take the player's score over 21). Jacks, Kings and Queens all count as 10. Other cards count as their face value. Suits are of no importance so a King and 6 count as 16; Jack and Ace count as 21; Queen and King count as 20; while 3 and 2 count as five.

The player now looks at his two cards. He may want to "stand" which means not draw any more cards; or he may want to "hit" which means to take another card. He can hit again if he so desires as well. When the player hits and the new card takes the player's total over 21 he has "busted" and the dealer wins the bet. If the player eventually stands then it is the dealer's turn to draw cards. The dealer is restricted to a simple strategy: he must draw cards to a total of 17, on which he must stand. A total over 21 busts the dealer.

If both dealer and player score less than 21, then the higher hand wins. If the scores are tied, it is called a "push" and no money changes hands. Winning hands are paid at even money except under the following circumstances:

If the player receives an Ace and a 10-valued card for his first two cards, and the dealer cannot match this, the player has a "blackjack" and is paid off at 3-2 .

The player may elect to "double-down." This enables the player to add a sum equal to his original bet to his wager. He must then draw one additional card only.

If the player receives two same-valued cards, then he may "split" them. In exchange for putting up a sum equal to his original wager, he gets two hands to draw from, both beginning with the identical cards he was first given. He plays each hand against the dealer's hand in the normal manner.

In addition, the player is allowed to make an "insurance" bet of no more than half of his original wager when the dealer is dealt an Ace. If the dealer matches the Ace with a 10, the player is paid 2-1 on his insurance bet, which loses otherwise.

Chapter 2

Basic Strategy and Beyond

Prior to the 1950s, blackjack play was based largely on guesswork. Analysis of the recommended advice of individuals regarded as card experts at the time, such as John Scarne, has revealed it to be little better than the strategies of the typical player, which yields a two percent advantage to the house.

A two percent casino advantage means the player would expect to lose two average bets every 100 hands in the long run. So, if he were betting $20, he would lose $40 every hundred hands. In the real world, the losses would not be smooth; some runs would heavily favor the player and some runs would heavily favor the house, but over millions of hands, the player would realize a two bet per 100 hand deficit on average.

The first attempt to discover the best strategy for blackjack was conducted in 1954 at Los Alamos. It used a simulation approach, with millions of hands being played on an IBM 701 computer in order to determine the correct playing decision for every total of cards. This attempt showed that the house had a 0.7 percent edge in the game of blackjack at the time over a player using what was then considered the best strategy.

In 1956 four US scientists, Roger Baldwin, Wilbert Cantey, Herbert Maisel, and James McDermott, working at an army base in Maryland, published a paper entitled *The Optimum Strategy in Blackjack*. The four men had spent three years analyzing every possible playing option in blackjack for every set of dealer and player upcards, in an attempt to figure out the best strategy. Apart from a few insignificant errors, they succeeded. There was little interest in the paper because they admitted the strategy would still lose money in the long run (0.6 percent per $100 wagered or 60 cents). Still the "basic strategist" would lose at a much slower rate than other players.

Apart from a few minor changes, this strategy has endured to the present day. There is one (and only one) set of correct rules for hitting, standing, doubling, or splitting in a given blackjack game. Basic strategy alters slightly with different rules or numbers of decks, but once you have established those rules the basic strategy for that game must be adhered to. To do otherwise is simply to lose more money.

As stated, there is only one basic strategy for any particular game. But there are many games with subtle rules variations. The following is a typical strategy for a six-deck game, by far the most common in the world right now.

Basic Strategy

Number of Decks: Six
S17: Dealer stands on Soft 17 (Ace, 6).
DA2: Player may double on any first two cards.
No DAS: No double after splits allowed.
NS: No surrender allowed.

Splitting Pairs

Your Cards	\multicolumn{10}{c}{Dealer's Upcard}

Your Cards	2	3	4	5	6	7	8	9	T	A
(A, A)	Y	Y	Y	Y	Y	Y	Y	Y	Y	Y
(T, T)	N	N	N	N	N	N	N	N	N	N
(9, 9)	Y	Y	Y	Y	Y	N	Y	Y	N	N
(8, 8)	Y	Y	Y	Y	Y	Y	Y	Y	Y	Y
(7, 7)	Y	Y	Y	Y	Y	Y	N	N	N	N
(6, 6)	N	Y	Y	Y	Y	N	N	N	N	N
(5, 5)	N	N	N	N	N	N	N	N	N	N
(4, 4)	N	N	N	N	N	N	N	N	N	N
(3, 3)	N	N	Y	Y	Y	Y	N	N	N	N
(2, 2)	N	N	Y	Y	Y	Y	N	N	N	N

Key:
Y = Yes, split the pair   N = No, don't split the pair

Soft Totals

Your Cards	2	3	4	5	6	7	8	9	T	A
(A, 9)	S	S	S	S	S	S	S	S	S	S
(A, 8)	S	S	S	S	S	S	S	S	S	S
(A, 7)	S	Ds	Ds	Ds	Ds	S	S	H	H	H
(A, 6)	H	D	D	D	D	H	H	H	H	H
(A, 5)	H	H	D	D	D	H	H	H	H	H
(A, 4)	H	H	D	D	D	H	H	H	H	H
(A, 3)	H	H	H	D	D	H	H	H	H	H
(A, 2)	H	H	H	D	D	H	H	H	H	H

Dealer's Upcard header applies to both tables.

Key:
H = Hit   S = Stand   D = Double; if you cannot, Hit
Ds = Double; if you cannot, Stand

Hard Totals

Dealer's Upcard

Your Cards	2	3	4	5	6	7	8	9	T	A
17	S	S	S	S	S	S	S	S	S	S
16	S	S	S	S	S	H	H	H	H	H
15	S	S	S	S	S	H	H	H	H	H
14	S	S	S	S	S	H	H	H	H	H
13	S	S	S	S	S	H	H	H	H	H
12	H	H	S	S	S	H	H	H	H	H
11	D	D	D	D	D	D	D	D	D	H
10	D	D	D	D	D	D	D	D	H	H
9	H	D	D	D	D	H	H	H	H	H
8	H	H	H	H	H	H	H	H	H	H

Key:

H = Hit   S = Stand   D = Double; if you cannot double, Hit

European Basic Strategy

The European (no–hole-card) basic strategy differs from the American one in the following situations:

A-A vs. dealers A hit (instead of split)

8-8 vs. A hit (split)

8-8 vs. 10 hit (split)

11 vs. A hit (double or hit depending on the number of decks)

11 vs. 10 hit (double)

Splitting strategy when DAS is allowed

2-2, 3-3, 7-7 split vs. dealers 2, 3, 4, 5, 6, 7
4-4 split vs. 5, 6
6-6 split vs. 2, 3, 4, 5, 6
8-8 split vs. 2, 3, 4, 5, 6, 7, 8, 9
9-9 split vs. 2, 3, 4, 5, 6, 8, 9
A-A split vs. all except A

Doubling down strategy D9 (no soft doubling)

Double 11 vs. 2, 3, 4, 5, 6, 7, 8, 9
Double 10 vs. 2, 3, 4, 5, 6, 7, 8, 9
Double 9 vs. 3, 4, 5, 6

Soft-hands strategy when doubling not allowed

A-7 stand vs. 2, 3, 4, 5, 6, 7, 8 and hit vs. 9, 10, A
A-6 and lower always hit, except always split A-A

There are slightly different basic strategies for each game but learning each puts a strain on the memory and does not significantly change your monetary expectation. The one exception is the single-deck game. Complete basic strategy for the single-deck game is presented in Appendix C and should also be learned.

Rules

Here is how to calculate how much advantage the house has over you with basic strategy. Start with a value of

+0.02 percent for single deck, S17, DOA, 3:2 BJ Payoff and adjust that value according to the following table:

Rule	% Change in Edge
S17: dealer stands on soft 17	
DOA: player may double on any first two cards	
H17 (dealer hits soft 17)	-0.19
Late Surrender (LSR)	+0.02 SD
	+0.07 shoes
Early Surrender (ESR)	+0.62–0.71*
two decks	-0.35
four decks	-0.5
six decks	-0.6
DAS (double after split allowed)	+0.13
double on 10 & 11 only (D10)	-0.26
	-0.13 shoes
double on 9, 10, 11 only (D9)	-0.13
	-0.06 shoes
double on three or more cards	+0.24
resplit Aces (RSA)	+0.02
21 pushes Dealer 10 up BJ (P21)	+0.15
six card automatic win	+0.11
drawing to split Aces	+0.14
2:1 BJ Payoff	+2.32

* Depends on other rules

Simply adding and subtracting the figures for these rules is a fairly effective way of estimating the basic-strategy house advantage. (However, it is just an estimate. The values of some rules impact each other, creating minor effects difficult to calculate exactly without a computer simulation.)

Note that if you are going to play blackjack you must forget about extra-sensory perception, hunches, astrology, and other superstitions. The above strategy will always give you the correct play for every hand assuming you are not memorizing the cards. Sometimes players look at the basic strategy and say things like "I would never double down my 9 against a 3" or "I would not hit my 16 against a 10 because I will always bust." This thinking may be reinforced by a session of play where they tried hitting 16 against a 10 and always lost. From time to time this will happen for two reasons. Firstly, 16 vs. 10 is a losing situation whatever you do, so hitting merely makes you lose less often. Secondly, the right play will often appear to be the wrong one. This is because short-term luck rewards bad players with occasional periods of success and punishes good players with periods of failure. Over time things will even out and the player who uses basic strategy will do better than the uninformed player.

There are complex mathematical reasons why each play is correct. Some plays, such as the aforementioned 16 vs. 10 or hitting A-7 vs. 9 go strongly against human instinct. Sometimes blackjack experts attempt to explain to bad players why a certain play is correct. My explanation is simple: the computer says so.

Chapter 3
Card Counting I
Edward O. Thorp; A Simple Winning System; How to Practice Card Counting

Card counting is an advanced gambling tool, which could in theory give the player an advantage in almost any gambling game using cards. Card counting relies on a very simple theory. Sometimes cards which are good for the player are dealt out and many cards which are favorable for the dealer remain, giving the dealer an advantage. Sometimes there is a balance of cards good for both player and dealer dealt out and no one has an advantage. Sometimes cards which are good for the dealer are dealt out, which leaves many player-favorable cards, giving the player an advantage. If we bet more when we have the advantage and less we do not, then we will win more than the dealer in the long run. It is that simple.

Card counting depends upon knowledge of the undealt cards. Once dealt, cards are put into the discard tray and do not reappear until the pack is shuffled. This changes the odds. For example, if there are no Aces left in the shoe, the player cannot get a blackjack. While the dealer cannot either, the player gets paid 3-2 on his blackjack, but the dealer only gets even money. Obviously the missing Aces do not help the player because he can't get that 3-2 payoff, but do help the dealer since he doesn't have to make any 3-2 payoffs.

But what if no Aces appear after half the deck is dealt? Then surely the player must have an increased chance of a blackjack? This simple idea occurred to a small elite of card hustlers in the pre–World War II years in Nevada. They would raise their bets dramatically after a glut of small cards appeared, from the minimum amount permitted at the table to the maximum.

This idea first appeared in print in 1944 in *MacDougal on Dice and Cards*. The author, Micky MacDougal, was a special investigator for the Nevada gaming control board. MacDougal was something of a hero, renowned for combating the rampant cheating of a Las Vegas then controlled by the mob. His work has sadly passed into history. Yet, he was the first to sense that tracking the cards could influence the monetary outlook of the players.

But full-blown card counting was developed in the 1950's by Dr. Edward O. Thorp. Let's take a brief look at the career of this gambling genius.

Edward O. Thorp

Professor Thorp is a character so extraordinary that had he not really lived, somebody would have created him for a novel. Unquestionably the greatest mind ever to turn itself to the invention of gambling systems, Thorp made small fortunes at blackjack in trips to Vegas and Puerto Rico in the 1960's, enlisting the help of a shadowy crossroader and a millionaire, known only as Mr. X and Mr. Y. Despite his success, "I could have made $300,000 a year at that game," Thorp was reluctant to pursue a career as a card sharp and wrote his seminal *Beat the Dealer* (Random House, 1962) outlining his winning method instead.

This blackjack work brought him into contact with information theorist Claude Shannon, and discovering a shared interest in gambling, they began developing a space-age device to predict the path of a roulette ball in order to accurately predict where the ball would land. After some initial success the project was abandoned owing to technical difficulties. Thorp then hooked up with one William Walden and turned his attention to the sophisticated card game of baccarat, devising and testing a count system to beat certain side bets that were available at that time. After they cleared several thousand dollars, Thorp and a trained team of accomplices found themselves roughly ejected from the casino.

Thorp then turned his attention to the greatest gambling game of all, pioneering the incredibly successful "warrant-hedging" technique on the stock market. The approach exploited pricing inefficiencies, "locking in" guaranteed profit. The method was recorded for posterity in his now out-of-print classic *Beat the Market*.

Over 65 *billion* dollars has passed through Thorp's hands over the last few decades, and his personal fortune can only be guessed at.

Thorp publishes an occasional paper on blackjack every few years or so and keeps some connections with the gambling subculture. Almost as an afterthought, in the last few years, he experimented with a sports betting system and, after relieving Las Vegas of an obscene amount of money, and apparently bankrupting one casino in the process, returned to investment. Judged by any criteria, Thorp is without a doubt the most successful gambler who ever lived. All of this was due to an extraordinary ability to devise practical systems to turn chance to his advantage.

Thorp and Card Counting

While a student, Thorp became interested in a technical mathematical paper on blackjack (known as the "Baldwin basic strategy"), as he had been toying with the idea of escaping poverty with a scientific gambling system. Experimenting

with the recommended strategy at the casino, he was surprised to find that it appeared to work; his plays seemed
superior to those of his more experienced fellow players who
followed their gamblers' instincts. The strategy gave him an
almost dead-even gamble with the house. Fascinated, he considered if there might have been a way actually to turn the
odds in the player's favor.

The Baldwin paper had recommended playing according to a strategy that was correct for a full deck of cards. Of
course, when playing blackjack the cards are dealt out and
placed in a discard pile, and will not reappear until the shuffle. With access to a primitive computer Thorp experimented
by instructing the machine to see what happened when decks
with certain ranks of cards were removed.

He discovered that the removal of low cards (2s
through 7s) gave an advantage to the player, while the
removal of high cards (9s, 10-values, Aces) favored the house.
Also, with certain cards removed, the correct playing strategy
altered. Thorp figured this knowledge could be used to actually beat the casino at its own game. By betting more when
many cards favoring the player remained, and the table minimum when cards favoring the dealer remained, the player
would bet most of his money when the advantage was with
him and slowly grind out a victory. This advantage could be
increased by using knowledge of the undealt cards to make
better decisions on the play of each hand.

Thorp constructed his highly successful 10-count system which he used to win many thousands of dollars from the
casinos of Nevada and Puerto Rico. Thorp's disciples who
learned the strategy from the best-selling *Beat the Dealer*, tried
their own luck with his system. When the casinos realized
what was happening, they retaliated with a host of countermeasures designed to thwart the "counters." Thorp's system,
while complex, was significantly more powerful than the
crude prototype systems developed by the pre-war card hustlers.

The Theory Behind Card Counting

How does counting work in today's casinos? Well, the most popular systems are called "point counts." Cards are given a value according to how good or bad their removal is for the player. Cards whose removal from the deck are bad are given a minus value, good cards are given a plus value. The counter at all times keeps a "running count" in his head, which begins at zero with a full deck. Every time he sees a card he adds or subtracts its value from the running count. When the running count is high (lots of low cards have been dealt out) he has an advantage. He divides by the number of decks remaining, to obtain what is called the "true count." If the true count is positive enough he will raise his bet.

The reason why the removal of cards causes an imbalance in the odds lies in the symmetrical nature of the game. The house's advantage at blackjack comes from one feature of the game only—the double-bust. When the player busts his hand, it is irrelevant if the dealer busts also, because the player loses! If the player plays exactly as the dealer does, hitting on 16 and standing on 17 and above, the "double-bust" would give the house an eight percent edge. This does not take blackjacks into account. Although the player and dealer can get blackjacks, the player is paid off at 3-2 while the dealer gets even money only. This reduces the house edge to 5.6 percent. The correct application of hitting, standing, splitting and doubling strategies whittles down the house edge to approximately 0.5 percent. The removal of high cards helps the dealer because it favors his crude hit/stand strategy. When he draws to a stiff hand, the appearance of a low card helps the dealer. This is true for the player also, but the player will not be drawing as frequently as the dealer since he can decide which stiff hands to hit and which to stand on.

High cards favor the player because:

1. They increase the possibility of a blackjack;
2. They increase the likelihood of a favorable result from double-downs and splitting (which the dealer cannot do);
3. The dealer is more likely to bust stiff hands with a 10.

Contrary to popular belief, you do not need to have a good memory to count cards. Most count systems require you to remember only one number at a time. Counting cards requires you only to perform simple addition and subtraction. The main difficulty is in doing this accurately and quickly in the face of intense pressure and scrutiny.

A Simple Winning System

The easiest winning system is known as the "Ace-5 count" first published by the American blackjack millionaire Ken Uston. It captures roughly half the available gain from the systems used by the professionals, though it is considerably easier to use. All you do is this: Every time you see an Ace come out of the pack, count -1. Every time you see a 5, count +1. The higher the count, the greater your advantage. Bet your money according to the RC (running count), as follows:

RC	Units
under +3	1
+3	2
+4	3
+5	4
+6	6
+7	8
+8	12

In a six-deck game where a deck or less is cut out of play, this will get you a small edge over the house. I strongly recommend, however, that you leave the table when the running count becomes extremely negative. When the count is negative you are playing at a greater disadvantage than you would be off the top of the deck, and the less you play in such a situation the better. Ideally you would leave whenever the count went below 0, but this is impractical as it would mean leaving the table too often. Try leaving at -2 or -3. This will help you win a little more.

I do not recommend you use this system in a six-deck game but if you do, be aware that a large spread is needed to make a consistent profit (1-16 at least) or you must leave the table frequently.

Do not expect to get rich with this system. Your average rate of profit is only a small fraction of what you're betting. Your fluctuations (the up and down swings) will be wild in both directions. But once you have learned this system, you can play in any casino in the world and know you have the advantage over the house, and you will be playing the game better than 99 percent of all other players!

You must play perfect basic strategy to use the Ace-5 system. If you do not, you will be raising your bet when you do not have an advantage and will end up losing money.

But there are much better count systems available that can give you even higher edges.

A typical count system, used by a majority of expert players, is called the Hi-Lo. It looks like this:

Ace	10	9	8	7	6	5	4	3	2
-1	-1	0	0	0	+1	+1	+1	+1	+1

Again we add or subtract one, according to the value given each time we see a card (ignore the card if value = 0) and keep a running count in our heads just as with Ace-5.

This time we divide the running count by the number of decks remaining. This is called the True Count. The True Count (TC) is used to determine whether you or the casino has the advantage. When the TC is 0 you have a disadvantage of 0.5 percent. Each TC point is worth approximately 0.5 percent. A TC of +1 gets you even with the house, while a TC of -1 gives you a disadvantage of one percent. A TC of +2 is where the game becomes interesting: the card counter now has an advantage of 0.5 percent over the house, large enough to justify a bet increase.

A typical betting schedule (one which I have used) looks like this:

TC < 2	Minimum bet
TC = 2	Two units
TC = 3	Four units
TC = 4	Eight units
TC ≥ 5	Twelve units

In addition to using the count for bet sizing, counters alter the play of their hands from basic strategy according to the count. Basic strategy is designed for a full deck of cards. When there are excesses or deficiencies of certain cards, the best strategy is different. The most important play is to take insurance at a True Count of +3 or higher. I also recommend you play these hands differently according to the count:

Your hand	Dealer's card	If count is. . .	Action
Insurance		≥ +3	Take Insurance
16	10	≥ 0*	Stand
15	10	≥ +4	Stand
12	3	≥ +2	Stand
12	2	≥ +4	Stand
9	2	≥ +1	Double
9	7	≥ +4	Double
16	9	≥ +5	Stand
13	2	≥ 0	Draw
12	4	≥ 0	Draw
12	5	≤ -1	Draw

Your hand	Dealer's card	If count is. . .	Action
12	6	≤ -1	Draw
13	3	≤ -2	Draw
11	A	≥ +4	Double
10	10	≥ +4	Double
10	A	≥ +4	Double
10, 10	5	≥ +5	Split
10, 10	6	≥ +5	Split
15	9	≥ +3	Surrender
15	10	≥ 0	Surrender
15	A	≥ +2	Surrender
14	10	≥ +4	Surrender

* This requires a little explanation, as students often remark that this index makes no sense, since this contradicts basic strategy, which is correct with a full deck. The reasoning is complicated: these indices are derived by determining an average of the correct indices at each deck level. Some plays may require a decision at a certain TC with two decks remaining and a slightly higher TC with one deck remaining. For convenience an average number derived from every deck level is used. Off the top of the deck you should always hit with a 16 vs. 10, but as more and more cards are dealt out a TC of 0 comes to favor standing. Overall, standing with a count of 0 wins more money than hitting. These figures have been optimized for the six-deck game.

Most blackjack books will tell you how to use the count to vary the play of many more hands. With the possible exception of the single-deck game I do not agree it is necessary to know more strategy changes than those I've listed above. Most advice to the contrary was written before it was understood how little play departures from the basic strategy actually contribute to your edge. Credit goes to Don Schlesinger, author of *Blackjack Attack* (RGE Publishing), for the discovery that the indices in the first 18 lines of the table above contribute most of the gain from strategy variation. Schlesinger christened them "The Illustrious 18."

The last four plays in the table, known as the Fab Four, are for the late surrender rule. This is an infrequently offered rule that allows the player to give up half his bet after seeing his first two cards in exchange for not having to play out his hand. Surrender is not allowed when the dealer has a black-jack, in which case the whole bet is lost.

Surrender is a rule of little importance to a basic strate-gist, but quite valuable to a card counter since surrender is often the correct play when a card counter makes larger bets. If you use a different count the plays you will use (and of course the index numbers) may be slightly different. But this will be of no great significance.

Finally, when approximately a deck has been cut off, the significance of each play changes. The higher count strat-egy departures such as 15 vs. 10 benefit from deeper penetra-tion and conversely suffer when fewer cards are dealt.

Styles of play can change the important numbers as well. For the backcounter who plays only when the count is positive, for example, 16 vs. 10 is irrelevant. The backcounter always stands: if the count recommended hitting he wouldn't be at the table.

Easy Play Strategy

For the player who counts and varies the bet size, but does not want to learn how to vary his playing strategy, then it is still possible to gain a little over basic strategy without memorizing indices. Because more money is bet at higher counts, use a slightly different basic strategy. Whenever an index recommends changing strategy at a TC >0 or +1 then change your basic strategy, always making the decision as if there was a TC>0 or +1. For example, you would always stand with 16 vs. 10. This gets you a little extra gain for virtu-ally no extra effort. It will work with all count systems which count small cards as plus and 10s as minus. This is not a replacement for learning the full set of figures, however, as it will generally not contribute more than .05 percent to your advantage.

Number of Decks

For the card counter the number of decks used is crucial information. All other things being equal, fewer decks are much more favorable. But other things are not necessarily equal. The casinos are aware that fewer decks are counter-friendly and "sweat" high action closely. Moreover they may take greater precautions, such as reducing the percentage of cards dealt out. Multiple decks can be beaten with back-counting and a large spread. It is not wise to play every hand at six-deck, as the negative shoes can prove never-ending. However, when the count goes positive, you will have a greater number of hands to play on average before the shuffle. One advantage of multiple decks is that they generally have higher limits so greater *absolute profits* can be realized.

Mathematically, fewer decks are always better for the player. Flat betting a typical single-deck game is more favorable than spreading from 1 to 20 units in a typical eight-deck game.

The primary reason most new counters fail is that they do not use the necessary bet spread to beat the game they play against, often because they were introduced to classic texts whose advice was intended for the much more favorable games of yesteryear, where little or no bet variation was required to win consistently.

The bare minimum bet spread is 2 x N, where N is the number of decks. Anything less and the game is at best marginally profitable.

Which Seat Should I Sit In?

The position you sit in has little effect on your winnings except at hand-held games. Mathematically it is best to sit in the seat furthest to the right, known as "third base," because you can see all the cards dealt to any other players before making your own playing decisions. The more information you have about the other cards, the more accurate your play will be. But this effect is negligible for six-deck and irrelevant for eight-deck.

Moreover some pit bosses treat third base as an "expert position," where a card counter would automatically sit. They may have gained this impression from reading older literature on blackjack where third base provides a significant advantage to a card counter in the single-deck games still to be found in Las Vegas. The small gain to playing strategy is not worth the extra heat in this instance. Sometimes a player in the "first base" position (the seat farthest to the left) may see a card that is about to be dealt when a sloppy dealer exposes it. Obviously, when this happens, first base is the best place to sit. Most counters choose their seat solely on the basis of comfort.

Penetration

Penetration refers to how many cards are dealt out of the pack before the shuffle, and is typically referred as a percentage of the total number of cards. While penetration is of no importance to the player who plays only basic strategy, it is of great importance to the card counter. In fact, it is the most important thing to a card counter apart from the number of decks.

The number of cards cut out of play should ideally be no more than a deck in a six-deck game, and anything less than a deck is excellent. While one-and-a-half decks might be okay with a large spread, anything less and it's better not to play. It is essential to scout around for good penetration. To illustrate its importance, the four-deck player wins three times as much with half a deck cut out of play as he does with a deck and a half cut off. This is due to the fact that favorable opportunities occur with increasing frequency as more cards are dealt out, and gains from strategy variation increase also. A few extra hands are much more important in terms of the money you can expect to make than the difference between the strongest and weakest commercial counting systems.

Number of Players

Card counters like to play alone. There is a reason for this. Having other players at your table slows the pace of the game down. The slower the game the fewer hands you will play. The fewer hands you play, the less money you will make. Even the best games can be a waste of time at a full table. Heads-up, or solo play against the dealer, is perfect for a card counter.

Never play shoe games with more than three players at a table.

You may often have difficulty finding a table which is not full at a hand-held game, and there are special strategies for single-deck games such as depth-charging, which can exploit a game with many players. However, all other things being equal, the fewer players the better.

Backcounting

Backcounting is a very powerful card-counting technique which, in the opinion of many professionals, is the only way to play the multiple-deck game. It is also known as Wonging, after Stanford Wong, the man who first popularized the technique. This involves counting down the cards as they are dealt, and only sitting down when the count is favorable. When the count goes bad the player gets up and leaves the table. Most back counters flat bet, since they always have the advantage when they play.

Because American casinos are often quite large, because "back betting" is quite a common practice, and because no bet variation is required, it is quite possible to backcount and get away without too much attention from the pit. The downside is that the tables are often either completely packed or empty, and taking a seat when you want one is not always possible.

When backcounting, it is important to observe the cards you *actually see*, rather than the cards that are dealt. Cards that are not seen should not be counted, and you should treat them as if they are behind the cut card. If three decks of a six-deck shoe have been dealt but you did not see any of them, you should divide your count by six, not by three. In fact, because this is like playing a game with 50 percent penetration, you would probably not waste your time observing this game unless the table was flooded with small cards. In general you should backcount from the beginning of the shoe.

Leaving the table is an easier matter. If you do this in the small hours you can flit from table to table looking like a player trying to find a hot dealer. You cannot do this too much. I would recommend leaving the table at counts of -1 or below.

Skilled backcounters practice the ability to scan a table full of cards in less than three seconds. There are numerous subtleties involved. Some specialists perfect the ability to scan cards via casino mirrors. Others develop their peripheral vision (one simple trick—looking down enhances peripheral vision). My own favorite technique is to play another game entirely, such as roulette or baccarat, for small stakes, casing the deck as I do so. Even if I cannot see the cards, and my eyesight is not what it was, I can infer certain things from a distance from the actions of the players. A player who stands on a two-card total, for example, is more likely to have a hand composed of high cards, it is not not essential to know what the cards actually are.

How to Practice Counting

The training methods recommended to learn card counting have varied little with time. To begin with, it is imperative that you know basic strategy *perfectly*. You will need to concentrate fully on learning to count cards and you cannot afford to be distracted by having to remember borderline basic strategy plays. Basic strategy should come to you without conscious effort.

To start, take a full deck of cards and drop them down on a table in front of you, one by one. Count them as you do so, and recite this value out loud. To save time, say "m" instead of minus. At this stage, precision is more important than speed, which will come with time. Your count should always end up with a value of zero—if it does not you have erred in your count. If you have counted the cards correctly, you should be able to predict the value of the last card to be dealt to some extent. If your count after the penultimate card is -1, you know the final card must be a 10 or an Ace. If it is +1, you know the final card is a 2-6. If you have a count of zero, you know the final card must be of value 7-9. Continue to do this until you can count down the deck 19 times out of 20 with complete accuracy. Then you can concentrate on improving your speed.

The generally accepted benchmark for counting down a full deck is 25 seconds or less. If you cannot count this fast, you will struggle in a casino.

In addition you should be able to spread out 20 cards in front of you and count their value in 7 seconds or under. This is equivalent to counting the cards on a full table.

Now, get four decks of cards (or six if you prefer) and begin to play blackjack against yourself as in the casino. To start with, concentrate on keeping an accurate running count and playing basic strategy. Do not raise your bet or attempt strategy deviations. Cut off a deck of cards, just as the casinos do. When you have counted through the cards, check through the discards quickly. Their combined value should equal zero. When you have done this successfully several times, try converting the running count to the true count and betting accordingly with matchsticks or chips. For most people, this is the most difficult part to learn.

There are some shortcuts that can make it easy however. Every hand that is played uses up 2.7 cards on average and therefore 10 x 2.7 is close to enough to a half-deck for our purposes. Every 10 hands, or every five rounds of heads-up play against the dealer, you know that roughly another half-deck is gone, and you can adjust your true count accordingly. You do not need to know anything more than the number of half-decks that remain that is quite good enough. Even a rough guess of how many hands, and therefore half-decks, have been played is quite accurate. One method I have used in heads-up play is to press one finger into each palm with each round that is played (when in the casino you must do this out of sight). When I get to the thumb I know a half-deck has been used up. Of course, another player entering the game complicates this method.

Most other texts on counting recommend that you estimate the number of decks remaining by looking at the discard tray. I don't do this: it looks too obvious, as ordinary players take no interest in the discard tray. Moreover, it is difficult to estimate the number of decks remaining visually with the same accuracy as the hand-counting method.

If you prefer to eyeball the stack rather than count the number of hands, you must purchase cards which are the same as those used in the casinos (you can find these in magic shops). Mix several packs together, tear out handfuls of cards and estimate their number. Then count the number of cards in the handful to determine how close you were. Try to get consistently within twenty cards.

Perhaps the best way to estimate the remaining cards is to count hands and confirm your estimate with peripheral vision of the discard tray. Counting hands is more often the best method when part of the deck has been dealt, yet it is often easier and quicker to estimate visually the number of decks remaining at the beginning and towards the end of the pack, particularly when a deck or less remains.

Finally, when you can play basic strategy, count and bet according to the TC perfectly, try varying the play of your hands with the count. Learn the variations one at a time. The first two plays, 16 vs. 10 and 15 vs. 10, are far more important than the others. It is vital you deviate from these basic strategy plays with clinical accuracy before you learn the other indices. Use whatever tricks help you. For example, you know not to stand whenever you have a 15 vs. 10 if you have less than your largest bet out. You don't need to convert the true count to know when to stand with a 16 vs. 10, you just need to know whether the running count is positive or negative. And so on.

If you are going to use deviations from basic strategy (and this is not essential since most of your gain comes from bet variation), then you must be correct. It is better to play basic strategy than to deviate mistakenly from basic strategy.

The whole process of learning a professional system takes several months at the least. It is often frustrating and discouraging. Once you have learned to count you will need to practice continually. Just playing is not enough. Some errors do not manifest themselves while in the casino and become embedded in your play. Only by dispassionately analyzing your play and by continually going back to the charts and testing yourself, can you be certain your play is correct.

Chapter 4
Card Counting II
Systems Compared

I have made the Table which follows, showing the most common strategies along with values for their betting, playing and insurance performance. These values are called Playing Efficiency, Betting Correlation, and Insurance Correlation. They measure how close a system is to a "perfect" system, one which would obtain the maximum possible gain from each area of play.

Playing Efficiency was defined by Peter Griffin, a mathematics professor and analyst of the game (see Chapter 10). Playing Efficiency is not relevant to unbalanced systems (systems that don't end up as zero when a deck is counted) and is only an estimate. Playing Efficiency and Betting Correlation do not include side counts. Ease of use is rated from 1 (hardest) to 10 (easiest) and is based strictly on my own opinions. Definitions follow.

Betting Correlation: This is how close a system is to a perfect betting count. The figure represents how much of the gain can be realized. The Hi-Lo count for example has an excellent 0.97 percent Betting Correlation. A perfect betting count would have a value of 1.00.

Playing Efficiency: This is how close a system is to a perfect playing system. No existing commercial system has a playing efficiency of more than 0.70 percent because commercial systems concentrate on the ratio of Aces and 10s to low cards, which is not the best information to have for all plays, particularly stiff hands. A computer might be able to tell you how many 5s and 6s are left when you have 16 vs. 10, but no count system will.

Insurance Correlation: This is how close a system is to a perfect insurance system.

Explanation of Counting Systems

Counting Correlation System	Counting Values										"Best" Efficiencies			
	2	3	4	5	6	7	8	9	X	A	Source	Play	Bet	Ins.
Ace-five	0	0	0	1	0	0	0	0	0	1	Uston	.09	.55	0
AOII (B)	1	1	2	2	2	1	0	-1	-2	0	Carlson	.67	.92(A)	.85
Canfield	0	1	1	1	1	1	0	-1	-1	0	Canfield	.63	.87	.76
CORE	0	1	1	1	1	1	0	0	0	0	Frank	.26	.63	.41
Griffin-1	0	0	1	1	1	1	0	0	-1	0	Griffin	.64	.84	.85
Heath	1	1	1	1	0	0	0	0	-1	0	Heath	.56	.86	.85
Hi-Opt I (C)	0	1	1	1	1	0	0	0	-1	0	Humble	.61	.88(A)	.85
Hi-Opt II (D)	1	1	2	2	1	1	0	0	-2	0	Humble	.67	.91(A)	.91
High-Low	1	1	1	1	1	0	0	0	-1	-1	Wong	.51	.97	.76
Ita (E)	1	1	1	1	1	1	0	1	-1	-1	Sys.Res	.53	.96	.69
KO (UB)	1	1	1	1	1	1	0	0	-1	-1	Fuchs / Vancura	.54	.98	.78
Lima (UB)	0	1	1	1	1	1	0	0	0	-1	May	.88	.65	.86
Mentor	0	1	2	2	2	2	0	0	-1	-1	Renzey	.58	.97	.80

Counting Correlation System	2	3	4	5	6	7	8	9	X	A	"Best" Source	Efficiencies Play	Bet	Ins.
Red 7(UB)	1	1	1	1	1	.5	0	0	-1	-1	Snyder	.54	.98	.78
Revere PC	1	2	2	2	2	1	0	0	-2	-2	Revere	.55	.99	.78
Revere APC	2	3	3	4	3	2	0	-1	-3	-4	Revere	.66	.93(A)	.85
Revere 14	2	2	3	4	2	1	0	-2	-3	0	Revere	.65	.92(A)	.82
Unbal 10s	1	1	1	1	1	1	1	1	-2	1	Roberts	61	.73	1.00
Uston +/-	0	1	1	1	1	1	0	0	-1	-1	Uston	.55	.95	.76
Uston APC	1	2	2	3	2	2	1	-1	-3	0	Uston	.69	.91(A)	.90
Wilson	-1	-1	-1	-1	-1	-1	-1	-1	1	4	Wilson	.31	.80	.45
Wong Halves	1	2	2	3	2	1	0	-1	-2	-2	Wong	.56	.99	.72
Zen	1	1	2	2	2	1	0	0	-2	-1	Snyder	.59	.96	.85
Ten Count	4	4	4	4	4	4	4	4	4	-9	Thorp	.62	.71	1.00

Notes on individual systems:

(A) indicates an Ace side-count is used, meaning the Ace is counted 0 for playing purposes and as -1 for betting purposes. This improves performance but requires greater concentration.

(B)Also known as the Canfield Master System.

(C)Also known as Einstein

(D) Also known as Stepine

(E) Also known as Silver Fox and Green Fountain

(UB) Indicates the count is unbalanced, meaning it does not sum to zero. The figures for playing efficiency are not a very good guide when it comes to unbalanced systems and should be taken only as a very crude estimate.

Comparison of Systems

Systems are often classed by level. The level of a system is the highest value any card is assigned. The relatively new KO system is widely reckoned to have the greatest power of the level-1 systems, narrowly edging the Hi-Lo system which has been the most popular count system since its inception. For single-deck games, where playing decisions are more important, the Hi-Opt system is optimal, closely followed by Green Fountain.

The best level-1 system for one and two-deck games is Advanced Omega II. For many decks, the better insurance correlation of Hi-Opt II (insurance becomes more important with many decks) edges out the Omega system. Beyond this level the mental strain of play becomes overpowering. Very few players are using level-3 or higher systems, and even fewer will bother once they know exactly how little gain such strain brings them. The best level-3 systems barely outperform the best level-2 systems by a few hundredths of a percent.

Knowledgeable theorists may be surprised by the inclusion of the Lima system. The Lima system is the best level-1 system for playing your hands. It was originally intended to be used in this book but discarded owing to the fact that betting is so much more important than playing in the modern game.

Super-Counters
Beyond the Fourth Level

Players who wish to go even further than this do not have many obvious choices. The popular systems already achieve close to perfect betting, so to do significantly better you have to break the 0.70 playing efficiency barrier. To do this you must use a *multi-parameter* system. This means you have to keep more than one count at the same time. Some commercial systems recommend the use of an Ace side-count, since the Ace behaves like a small card for play purposes and like a high card for betting purposes.

But the focused mind can go further, at least in theory. Can a system of greater complexity push the boundaries further?

Bert Fristedt and David Heath published an article entitled "The Most Powerful Blackjack Strategy Devised" in *Winning Magazine*. This involves counting cards in three groups: 2, 3, 4, 5 were simultaneously counted against 6, 7, 8, 9, and 10-valued cards. The player was supposed to use a two-dimensional strategy chart for playing strategy while just using the regular Heath count for betting. The playing efficiency of the system is .75, which looks impressive until you appreciate that translates to a mere one-tenth of one percent in advantage! The Heath system barely outperforms the best commercial system in shoe games.

Peter Griffin approached the problem from another angle. He suggested enhancing the Hi-Opt I system with no less than five side counts. He presented his ideas to the First and Second International Conferences of Gambling and Risk-Taking in June 1974–75. Griffin's method yields 0.89 percent in playing efficiency. Extensive simulations by John Gwynn showed that Griffin's strategy did achieve 0.2 percent over existing systems with just an Ace side-count. But again virtually nothing improved in multiple-deck games. And the tables Griffin's method requires you to memorize are very extensive, added to the difficulty in remembering almost half the deck in actual play.

David Sklansky offered another suggestion in Gambling Times, August, 1977 with his article "Getting the Best Of It: The Key Card Concept—An Extra Edge At The Blackjack Table." Sklansky's approach is less methodical, as he suggested memorizing a few key rules to exploit knowledge of the cards above that of a simple count. For example, if you have just seen four sevens come out on the last round in a single-deck game, and you have 14 vs. 10, it is a good idea to stand, since a seven gives you a 21 and the dealer 17. The seven in this case is the key card. However, as Sklansky later clarified, the key-card concept is not an actual system, just a set of general guidelines that might be incorporated into a system.

Surprisingly, though the development of computers has made it much easier, no subsequent work of note has been published concerning multi-parameter systems.

Chapter 5
Blackjack Espionage

"I am not what I am." —Iago, Shakespeare's *Othello*

Left unharassed, the professional card counter should be able to grind out significant profits in the long-term. Unfortunately, because they fear the loss of the least revenue, the casinos take measures to prevent card counting. If, anywhere in the world, you are suspected of card counting, your play will be analyzed by surveillance operatives, usually from the eye-in-the-sky. If their suspicions are confirmed you will be subjected to a number of countermeasures, such as:

1. Increasing the number of cards cut out of play.
2. Restricting your bet size.
3. Being told that you are allowed to play any game except blackjack.
4. Being "asked" to leave the casino.
5. Being given a written warning and formally barred.
6. Being given notice that a return to the casino will result in your arrest for trespassing.

How much of a problem this is depends greatly on the individual. For the full-time player there is always the next casino, the next town, or even the next country. A barring from one casino is not of great significance if the world is your playground. For the casual player, one who may be tied down to a full-time job, and patronizes only a few local casinos, the problem is far more serious.

Most modern blackjack literature overemphasizes the problem of barring. Great importance is attached to the establishment of an "Act." This requires the card counter to assume a persona that would not normally be associated with the obsessive and intelligent characteristics of the card counter. This Act will not fool anybody who is familiar with card counting and is actually scrutinizing the counter's play. The Act is designed to prevent such scrutiny from ever happening. In general, the scrutinizing will only occur if the pit boss becomes suspicious of an individual's play, and requests confirmation from the eye-in-the-sky. A pit boss is naturally going to pay more attention to a middle-aged professorial type than a loudmouthed tourist, or a rich playboy, for example. Acts are fun. They allow you to play different characters and revel in your own deception, and they can be successful in throwing the pit off your trail.

If you adopt an Act you must not be half-hearted about it. You must be 100 percent committed to the character you have created. Often high stakes players become enamored with the possibilities inherent in disguises, some even employ makeup wizards to kit themselves out! In truth, the most successful acts can be accomplished by adopting subtleties of movement, mannerism and speech.

You must become the character you are playing. It is not enough to put on an accent. That is not convincing. Good actors, both in the casinos and on the stage, do not act from the neck upwards. Create your own character's history, friends, occupation, etc. You should never be asked a question you do not have an answer for. Moreover if you are not wrapped up in the lifestyle of your character, your body language will give you away in many small unconscious signals. Other people pick up on this without realizing it and become suspicious without even knowing why. Pay attention to details such as the way you walk, sit, slouch and signal. These can give you away.

Another method of avoiding detection involves making "Cover Plays," which are plays not in accordance with the recommended actions of a card-counting system. This may mean making incorrect drawing, standing, splitting, and doubling decisions, not raising your bet when the count goes up and not lowering when it goes down, or occasionally betting high off the top of the shoe.

Forget about making cover plays if you play for small stakes. The reasons for this are simple: Your edge is small and you do not want to reduce it further. You will make incorrect plays from time to time in any case. You cannot make playing errors when you have large bets out, as the cost is too high, and your profit depends on these large bets. This is precisely when the pit will be watching you closely.

My opinion concerning the necessity of cover is simple. While the expert card counter plays blackjack against the dealer, he plays *poker* against the pit; that is, his play is geared towards the intelligence of the pit personnel. Against incompetent or disinterested casino personnel the counter plays *tight*, i.e. in accordance with the precise recommendations of his system. Against personnel skilled in the art of game protection he plays tight and loose; that is, he mixes up his play between correct strategy and seemingly whimsical or random play. He is always keeping the pit guessing but plays close enough to the dictates of the system to win consistently. I look at this method of survival in game-theoretical terms: it is the *optimal strategy*, that is, the best possible strategy in the real world of casino play against any method the pit may use to confirm that you count cards.

Note that the poker analogy extends to the importance of body language. Game protection personnel are instructed to look for give-away mannerisms which mark out the professional card counter, much as an expert poker player can deduce the strength of his opponent's hand from subtleties of movement and behavior. Counters, even ones who put on a fairly good Act, have certain unconscious habits: They handle chips in a precise and skilled manner, they are often over-friendly, they stare at the pit boss. The lessons are clear. Handle your chips in a clumsy and awkward manner, do not interact with casino staff unless you can do it in a natural manner. By all means monitor the pit boss's behavior but do it with your peripheral vision.

In general, once the pit has identified you as a potential threat, they will look through the surveillance tapes for any record of your play they can find. These tapes are kept for a finite period, and they may be erased after a week. Your play will be thoroughly analyzed to determine if you are counting. According to a former counter catcher Max Rubin, who worked at the Mirage casino in Las Vegas, it typically required a hundred hands to determine if a player was or was not counting. Obviously this would be higher or lower depending on the correlation between the counter's play and perfect mathematical application of the card counting system.

It is evident that a player who travels from club to club, plays only 40 minutes at a time in each and does not return for a week to the same shift has a very good chance of falling through the system. Bryce Carlson, author of *Blackjack for Blood* (Compustar Press, 1998) and one of the great Lawrence Revere's most successful pupils, advises not returning to the same casino for a period of three months.

Part II

Advantage-Play Techniques

How to Become a Casino's Worst Nightmare!

Chapter 6
Advantage Play I
Scorched Baize and Black Chips; Card Steering; Card Sequencing; Shadow Play

Scorched Baize and Black Chips

So far we have dealt with the history and practice of winning blackjack. What you are about to read are methods previously known only to a small handful of high stakes professionals. These techniques are the most lethal weapons in the arsenal of the advantage player. Practiced correctly in the hands of disciplined professionals they will decimate the bottom line of a casino in a comparatively short space of time. A code of secrecy amongst high stakes world travelers has kept many of these methods secret. Apart from a few obscure technical texts in specialist journals they have never appeared in print—until now! These techniques are worth several hundred times the cover price of this book.

All these methods have one striking feature in common. They give you knowledge of a specific card. It is an astonishing fact that knowing when just one card will appear, even in an eight-deck game, is a passport to the casino kingdom's treasure city.

Card Steering

One method that has been kept in a shroud of secrecy is known as card steering. A textbook example of card steering is given below. It was related to me by a highly successful professional gambler and maverick theorist known to me only as the *Green Baize Vampire* who described the play as he organized it.

A team of three players would take over an empty table so they could play all the spots. The guy at first base had the uncanny ability to cut exactly 23 cards from the back of the shoe. The team would note the last card (bottom card) of the shoe (not very hard to do with a careless dealer) and then let this guy cut.

After he cut 23 cards off the back, the last card would now be the 23rd card out of the shoe. If it was an Ace or 10 they would play their first round hands so that the guy in the middle (the big bettor) would get the 23rd card for his first card on the second round.

The first base player would play one, two, or three hands depending on how many hits the dealer took in the first round. The big bettor would play $2,500 on the hand expecting the big card, and $500 on the two hands next to it (in case the cutter was off by one card). The others would bet $25. If it was a small card, they would then play their first round hands so that the dealer would end up with the card as his hole card for the second round.

The player at first would put $25 on the first hand and the player would put $25 on the last hand (again, in case the cutter was off by one card). The big bettor would play three hands of $1,000 with perfect knowledge of the hole card. We watched and fast-forwarded through this tape for about 10 shoes, the cutter only missed once (by one card). They were also under suspicion of using a computer and counting for the rest of the shoe. They won over a hundred grand in a couple of nights play and were barred.

Most houses will not permit only 23 cards to be cut from the back of the shoe, and will call for at least a deck.

Scouting is essential to find a casino which does not do this. Needless to say, after the casino took this hit and reviewed the tapes, they figured out what was going on. Cutting 23 cards from the back of a 6 deck shoe is very hard to do consistently but when a cutter can do it, the casino is in big trouble.

Most players believe that setting a minimum number of cards from either end will protect a casino from a card steering team. In fact there is a simple way around it. The cutter turns the cut card on its side and places one end at the edge of the pack. He then twists the other end so the cut card lodges in the pack, and pulls the other end around so the deck is broken at the point measured by the precise width of the cut card. Then the number of cards is counted out exactly till the bottom card is reached. The cutter then knows exactly how many cards will be dealt out before reaching the bottom card if he uses exactly the same maneuver later.

If executed clumsily, this can look a little suspicious. With practice, a cutter should be able to perform the cut faster than the eye can see. When you know an Ace will appear as your first card you have a 50 percent advantage. With a 10 you have a 13 percent advantage. When you know the hole card you have a 10 percent advantage. That is why card steering can be so rewarding for the player and so devastating for the casino.

Note that you don't need to be able to perform this trick with the precision of a diamond cutter or a brain surgeon to gain a huge advantage. Knowing an Ace or a 10 will appear in the next six cards is quite enough to assure long-term wins.

Card Sequencing

In May 1997 an article appeared in *Esquire* magazine by a journalist named Michael Angeli. He wrote about his experiences with a high stakes blackjack team. He exposed a method he called "The Hammer." Many readers were enthralled with Angeli's infectious prose style and the description of a fantastic coup carried out by the team. Many professional blackjack players wrote off Angeli's article as pure fiction. In fact it contained much that was true. Too much in fact. "The Hammer" was actually a combination of several methods: card counting, shuffle tracking, and card sequencing, a technique previously only known to a secret cabal of elite professional card players.

Sequencing is really a very simple idea. It originated around the turn of the century in an esoteric magic book by Charles Jordan and C. O. Williams. It was first applied to blackjack by Edward O. Thorp over 20 years ago in an obscure technical paper called "Non-random shuffling with application to the game of Faro." Unlike card counting, you can prove it works easily by a simple test.

When riffled perfectly, cards remain in the same order in close proximity, more frequently than pure chance would suggest. If, for example, the Ace of spades immediately follows the 3 of diamonds in the deck, after one riffle (or shuffle) the Ace will tend to be the second card away from the 3; another riffle will leave it four cards down and a third will leave it eight cards from its original position. (Turn two adjacent cards face up, shuffle the deck and see it work for yourself.) By memorizing three card sequences—usually three "key cards" preceding or surrounding the "target card" a sequence tracker can collect enough data to follow the progress of a given card through the casino shuffle procedure. Amazingly, this simple fact makes virtually every casino card game—including those not yet invented—vulnerable; and the returns can be spectacular.

Crucial information for a sequence tracker is the number of riffles. A single riffle is ideal although quite difficult to find; but they do exist in casinos where they use complex shuffles with many decks. If a dealer riffled perfectly there would be one card separating key and target card, three cards if there were two riffles, and seven cards if there were three riffles.

In practice, things are not that simple. Dealers do not shuffle perfectly. Generally, the sloppier the dealer, the more unpredictable he is. Amateur shuffles typically "clump" cards. The clean and precise riffle will leave the cards close to the perfect model. The term we use to describe a particular dealer's riffle is the dealer's signature. A typical dealer's signature might look like the following:

Chance of key card following target card (percent)	Number of cards between key and target
12	1
10	2
9	3
8	4
7	5
5	6

Further, some casinos use a method called *stripping*. This involves reversing the sequence of cards by holding a segment and taking cards from the top onto the table. This can lead to your key card being behind your target card. Fortunately stripping has to be very thorough to be completely effective at breaking up card sequences.

Ace locators use their knowledge by memorizing "key" or "signature" cards that go into the discard tray before an Ace, then watching for the appearance of the signature cards after the next shuffle, knowing that when they appear the Ace is not far behind, probably in the next one to six cards. They would then spread to three hands, each of which would be a big bet. For example, you see 5-club, Q-spade, A-heart go into the discard tray together. After the pack has been shuffled you see 5-club come out closely followed by Q-spade. You know that A-heart is not far behind. You spread to multiple hands since you know the Ace is likely to appear in a target zone of one to six cards with a high probability (depending on the number of riffles). The hand that gets the Ace has a 50–52 percent edge!

Because of the multiple hands and the possibility that the Ace may have vanished with the cut or from stripping, your total edge on the round is actually smaller. It is further reduced by the possibility that the dealer may get the Ace, which gives him a 36 percent edge. It is reduced further still in multiple decks because of the difficulty of recognizing distinct cards. One Queen of hearts looks very much like another.

Note that ideally your bets should be in descending order. This is because the more cards that are dealt the greater the chance that the sequence has not been maintained through the shuffle. Consequently it is less likely the Ace is separated from its signature card by six cards than by one.

Unlike card counting some training in advanced memory techniques is necessary before you will be able to locate Aces accurately. To track say, six Aces in a four-deck shoe, requires you to memorize the value and suit of eighteen cards. Even if you are only playing basic strategy that is an extraordinarily difficult feat given the pace at which the cards are dealt.

There are many popular books available on how to train your memory. The basic principle behind having a good memory is to make data lively, fun and personal, linking dry unconnected information with vivid and dramatic story-telling. You must first learn the house procedure for picking up cards. You can only do this by observation, so you learn the procedure by *visual* association. You must not think in terms of what happens to blackjacks, and what happens to bust cards. You must see it in your mind's eye as if watching a film.

There are two methods casinos use to pick up cards. The first is called lay and pay, where the cards are not picked up until every bet has been settled. The second is pick and pay where the cards on a given hand are picked up as soon as the wager they are deciding has been settled.

Ace location is a much better strategy for two or more players than one. If one player spreads to multiple big bets when he knows an Ace is coming, his partner can spread to multiple small bets and prevent the Ace from going to the dealer. To illustrate, if your key cards come out as the last cards of a round, you know to spread to three hands. Using the dealer signature in the example above you have a 43 percent chance of getting the Ace, which is roughly seven percent on each hand. But you do not have that much advantage because the dealer has an eight percent chance of getting the Ace, which all your three hands would have to face. If you have players sitting to your left who can take three hands this can be avoided.

There are other forms of card location that I am aware of such as:

1. **Playing adjustments:** To improve the play of their hands, some players have attempted to improve their playing decisions in games using crude methods. Cards such as 5s and 7s are keyed (these are most useful for stiff hands) and the appearance of their signature cards may indicate plays contrary to basic strategy (such as doubling hard 14 when you know a 7 is about to appear). I don't recommend this, except possibly in games where just one riffle is used. This method can be extremely dangerous in the hands of a neophyte. Some plays have extremely high volatility associated with them. An erratic dealer's signature might wipe out any advantage you gained with this method.

2. **Shorting the deck:** A small bettor who keys 5s and spreads to multiple hands benefits a partner by having him playing against a deck that has basically been shorted of 5s. Fives are the most powerful card for the dealer since he can hit all his stiffs (12-16) and make a pat hand. The Big Player plays with 0.5 percent advantage for every 5 shorted from each deck in play by the small bettor. This is an extension of

the card eating technique I discuss in Chapter Six and may be thought of as one of the safer forms of Ace location.

3. **Early anchor:** A table minimum bettor who sits at first base tracks 5s rather than Aces. The player will make strange deviations from basic strategy in order to steer a five into his partner's hand when this will help—often accompanied by. . .

4. **Late anchor:** A player who tracks 10s and whose intent is to worsen the dealer's hand. Again, both methods are somewhat risky and require a very high degree of prediction to be successful, since early and late anchor can usually only influence one or two cards with their hit/stand decisions.

Sequencing is generally used in combination with card counting. How you want to accomplish this is up to you. Some players use a conservative strategy of only raising the bet when the key sequence occurs in a high count. Some players maximize their winnings by betting when either count or sequence indicates an advantage. In truth, sequencing is more powerful than counting early in the pack, where the counting information is limited. Conversely the count should over-ride sequence information towards the end of the pack.

How Much of an Edge Does Card Sequencing Give You?

How powerful is this technique? As with card counting, finding out how much of an edge you have depends on many factors. A debate raged on the subject recently on Internet blackjack forums. During this debate, I asserted casually that, over a wide range of conditions, sequencing was superior to straight counting. One eminent theorist shot back with an elegant mathematical proof based on a single-deck shuffle, where a player could have a 2.1 percent edge per tracked Ace. Overall he stated that an advantage of 0.4 percent could be achieved by memorizing four Aces. I pointed out that this understated things because this approach was less risky than a traditional count strategy as the bet size was only changed from 1 to 2 units, and multiple decks are harder to mix up than one deck. Moreover, because there is only one type of each card in single-deck, you do not need to remember more than one key, so this 0.4 percent edge is obtainable by just remembering four cards, easier than the most simple of count strategies.

A skilled programmer joined the discussion stating that "perfect" Ace tracking in a six-deck game could yield a rather better 2.6 units per 100 hands. Moreover, with DAS, S17, no surrender, and 66 percent penetration this game was very difficult to beat with counting as the only method of attack.

There was universal agreement that Ace location is very powerful when combined with card counting.

It's my opinion that an estimated gain of one percent is roughly what the typical sequence player obtains. But this figure may vary widely from game to game. The majority of games are not worth tracking, the riffling is too thorough. On the other hand, the very best games where just one riffle is used may give you as much as 80 percent prediction of a card. Under such circumstances it is pointless talking about advantage, they might as well hand you the money! It's more a question of what you can get away with than what your edge is.

Fine Points

There are some finer points of location play. Try and keep a record of how many times your predictions are successful. Many pro players will try mentally to locate an Ace over a hundred times before actually playing it. Every dealer has a "signature" to some extent, and the more data you collect the more accurate it will be. Some teams will send in a minimum bettor to "clock" the dealer. This informant will come away and communicate the information to his confederates, who then analyze the data and send in a big money team.

It is important to watch closely as the dealer squares up the deck, as an uneven interleaving resulting from unskilled shuffling can mess up the prediction. A perceptive player can improve his accuracy greatly. Ace location is uncertain because of the minor subtleties of a dealer's riffle, but it is less uncertain if you can actually observe these subtleties and use the visual data intelligently.

This is stronger if you use it with your sequence information. For example, if it looks to you as if the dealer's shuffle has left many cards in the same initial sequence, and some of your key cards come out in the same initial sequence, it is likely that you are correct. You would now adjust your playing strategy to take advantage of the new prediction you have, or if you are unsure, simply abandon the game.

Shadow Play

Observing flashed cards without the dealer's help or collusion is not cheating. For example, good players train themselves to evaluate the shades of darkness or "blur intensities" of partially flashed cards (e.g., darker shades or more intense blurs indicate higher value cards—valuable information). If a player sees flashed cards without dealer collusion, he is not cheating since the same advantage is available to all players who choose to be equally alert. Alert players also watch for flashed cards as the dealer riffles, shuffles, and cuts.

Dealers who riffle or strip too high often expose cards to players in the third base position. Often you will be able to note the location of a card with a certain part of the pack, sometimes you will know its exact location. Approximately one in five dealers do this to some extent and can be read from at least one seat at the table. The particular vulnerability depends on the dealer. Sometimes this behavior can be induced by putting the dealer "on tilt" by a confrontational manner. Other dealers can only be read by low-stakes players, they subconsciously "tighten up" when big money hits the felt.

Another technique requires the player to sink low in his seat while watching the shuffle. As the dealer splits the pack and places the decks on top of one another, the player may able to see the bottom card of each segment as it is dropped. He can therefore gain a good idea of when that card is to be dealt. This assumes, of course, that the dealer breaks the pack into even segments, otherwise the predictions will be too rough. Interestingly enough, this and many other advantage-play techniques require a skillful dealer rather than a sloppy, amateurish or imprecise dealer. You should note down the average number of cards in a segment while utilizing this method as well.

With more than a hand's worth of error, the segments will be too uneven to give you useful information. If this is indeed the case, try obtaining the cut-card and aim for the approximate position of the card you have seen which gives you the greatest advantage. Locate the line of least resistance in this area by applying gentle pressure, and you will find that the natural break in the deck will allow you to locate the desired card with 100 percent accuracy.

Using these techniques successfully is not easy. The skilled shadow player will ascertain the value of three or four cards in what would be the blink of an eye to an ordinary mortal. Some magicians have the extraordinary ability to riffle a deck of cards and ascertain the value of the entire sequence of cards. Such an ability would be astonishingly profitable. Unfortunately, mental dexterity of that complexity is innate; it is a rare ability that cannot be learned.

However, our reading input appears to be physiologically limited by span of focus and speed of move-fixation. The average human eye can "see" a spot about three average words in diameter and can move and fixate about four times a second. The key is to eliminate "redundant" information. You can train yourself to do this by using a T-scope, a device that flashes random images for a split second. The T-scope is a film strip projector with a focal plane shutter in front of the lens. Use a film of individual cards; practice instant recognition, gradually increasing the shutter speed and then begin to include images of multiple and partially obscured cards You must fix your eyes as input devices and let data flow in at a very high rate without conscious thought.

Dealer selection is an essential part of shadow player. Most dealers do not expose cards. Naturally, it is a mistake made more often by novices that, left uncorrected, can remain indefinitely. Some shadow players can put a dealer "on tilt" by psyching out the dealer with an intense glare. A dealer who is angry or under pressure naturally cannot maintain full concentration on the task and will make more errors. In particular this may manifest itself with the dealer taking out his frustration on the cards, leading to high stripping or riffling.

Surprisingly, the complex shuffles used to foil card sequencing, and the many decks used to frustrate card counting, create ideal conditions for the shadow player. And, when he has found a game to exploit, the shadow player will win much faster than a sequence tracker, and much much faster than a garden-variety card counter. Here is why:

How to Bet When You Know a Certain Card Will Appear

The power to exploit a given card when you know it will appear is one of the most important concepts in blackjack. Very few players do this correctly. It is very important if you wish to become wealthy from blackjack.

Say that you know an Ace is coming. How do you bet? An Ace gives you a fantastic 50–52 percent advantage. How do you bet? The answer is that you should risk a huge 40 percent of your bankroll. Of course the casino won't let you do that, so bet the table maximum. With a 10 you have a 13 percent edge. You should risk 10 percent of your bankroll. Again this may mean betting table maximum.

Players find this very hard to accept. But very aggressive betting is called for when you have such a large advantage. It can be proven mathematically that to bet a lesser amount results in dramatically smaller profits, while to bet more results in too great a risk.

Chapter 7
Advantage Play II
Lawrence Revere; How Professionals Affect Ordinary Players; Dealer Errors

Lawrence Revere

Lawrence Revere, or Specks Parsons, or any one of the other multiple aliases this shadowy figure went under, was a true blackjack professional. Like Thorp, Revere was not only a great blackjack theorist, but the first of the great *practitioners*. He won over a million dollars from the casinos during his career. A bloodless and clinical professional, he acted as a double agent for both casino and players, extracting money from each, legitimately and illegitimately, with both a comprehensive understanding of the mathematics of blackjack and a consummate mastery of human psychology.

Revere, originally a dealer, developed a crude count system in the late 1950s. He developed several other systems of increasing power, most notably the Revere APC, and became universally known and feared throughout Vegas. He also plied his trade with increasing success in other parts of the world. Even after a universal barring, he remained based in Nevada. With the publication of his seminal *Playing Blackjack as a Business* (Carol Publishing), he became the foremost authority on blackjack, and at his behest neophyte counters flocked to his door.

Unfortunately, Revere was also the incarnation of duplicity. He would send his students out into the casinos with betting schemes designed to bankrupt the players through overbetting (a subject then barely understood). When they returned to Revere to ask for assistance he would test their skills by asking them to count down a deck of cards, and unbeknown to them he would remove a card, thereby causing the counter to believe he had made an error. Revere would then chide the player for his lack of concentration and encourage the player to pay for more lessons.

Revere was also something of a double agent. He had casino contacts and pulled off a number of collusion scams. He worked for the casino identifying counters, some of whom were his own students. Revere also trained the next generation of blackjack experts. Chief among them were two young men, Lance Humble and Bryce Carlson, the respective, and respected, authors of *The World's Greatest Blackjack Book* (Doubleday) and *Blackjack for Blood* (CompuStar Press).

Inspired by a copy of *Playing Blackjack as a Business*, Carlson rang up Revere while in Las Vegas, met with the master and wound up buying Revere's $200 14-count system. Carlson then shortly afterward challenged Revere on his understanding on a technical point, the existence of the complex "floating advantage" whereby the same true count can be more valuable the more cards are dealt. Carlson exposed Revere's lack of understanding of the subject, causing Revere to reply venomously "You know Bryce, a little knowledge can be a dangerous thing" to which Carlson responded, "Exactly!" The phone line went dead. The two counters later renewed their friendship but never spoke of their fallout again.

Humble's dealings with Revere were more serious. Affiliating himself too closely with the dark one, Humble was cheated out of his investment in a private game where he was bankrolling Revere. Severing his associations with Revere, Humble forged out on his own and developed the Hi-Opt I system, which was publicized in his own *World's Greatest Blackjack Book*. Revere publicly vilified Humble, denigrating the Hi-Opt system as inferior. In truth it was a much better combination of simplicity and power than Revere's own creations.

To this day the organization Revere spawned markets his advanced systems at the original $200 price tag. Even today the system is ludicrously overpriced. Revere's claims of a four percent edge are purely fictitious. Even in the heyday of the single-deck game, it was not practical to achieve that much of an advantage with any card counting system. However, the Revere point-count system, which came with *Playing Blackjack as a Business*, is a better combination of simplicity and power and is still used by many professionals.

Revere was a great man. A man created for a time when Las Vegas was still under the shadow of The Mob. Fortunately those days have passed into oblivion, as has Revere himself.

Exploiting Dealer Errors and Shady Practices

One little-mentioned technique for winning at blackjack involves looking around for a sloppy or novice dealer. It is sometimes the case that when dealing a five-card hand with multiple Aces the dealer miscounts and draws when his hand has already busted. When this mistake is pointed out to him, or he recognizes it himself, a common practice is to place the card drawn in error under the shoe ready for the first hand of the next round. Knowing what this card is gives you a huge advantage. (I have only seen this practice when the card drawn in error is a high card. The card is generally burned when it is low, as no one would accept a low card as their first card).

If you are not sitting at first base you cannot take advantage of this directly, but you may be able to "backbet" on that spot. Even if the first base player is quite bad, you will still have a large edge assuming the first card is a 10 or Ace. If you are playing at first base and you know the first card is an Ace, remember that you have almost a 52 percent advantage! If you know it is a 10 you have a 13 percent edge. A 9 is break-even and anything less is good for the dealer.

If you are getting an Ace, the correct strategy is, as stated, to bet 40 percent of your bankroll. This may sound like a lot, but it is the correct fraction of your bankroll to bet, and anything less is lost money. Usually this amount will be the table maximum.

Here are some interesting, though not recommended, techniques that have been mentioned to me. In the subdued lighting conditions some casinos are forced to operate in, it is often easy for dealers or players to mistake the value of chips. One very effective method involves finding a rookie dealer in a darkened corner of a high roller joint, and mixing up bets between red and black chips in the hope the dealer will confuse the two.

Some counters will play under what would ordinarily be dreadful conditions because of frequent dealer errors. Just one unearned payoff an hour makes a radical difference. The first thing you must do to exploit this is understand the game procedure thoroughly and be aware of the slightest deviation from it. The most important thing is that *you must never let any errors go against you*. Become expert at recognizing the value of multiple-card soft totals. Practice by stripping a deck of cards of 8s, 9s, and 10-valued cards. Deal out hands to yourself and call out their total as you do so. Then check your call. You may be surprised at your initial error rate. Many skilled dealers would be also.

There are other Machiavellian ways to induce dealer mistakes. The simplest way is to get another bet out immediately after you have busted your hand. If the dealer busts also she may accidentally pay out to the whole table, including your new bet. This works particularly well when there are multiple split hands everywhere. Sometimes avid splitters end up with cards spread out over into the next spot creating some confusion. The payout for such a hand may end up going to the wrong player.

Perhaps you have heard sports commentators refer to a player who is getting "into a rhythm." Sometimes they will refer to an opponent trying to break up this rhythm by slowing down the pace of play. This theory can be used to break the concentration of the dealer. Find out the optimum speed of the dealer and play at a rate that he will be uncomfortable with. After a few minutes he will begin to adjust to this new speed. So you will subtly speed up or slow down again.

Obviously dealers, like anyone else, find it more difficult to concentrate on the task at hand when they are distracted by some strong emotional or external phenomena. If a player is angry, if a player they find attractive is being flirtatious, if a player is being unnecessarily awkward and indecisive in the manner of his betting and playing signals, this may distract them from the task.

Distracting a harassed and busy dealer at a full table with inane conversation can have interesting results. The dealer will mentally emphasize the action he must perform in his head to drown out distractions. This often leads to overemphasis: the message is still firmly implanted in his mind even after the action has been performed. You might end up getting paid twice.

Another way some cheats work is to shove a high denomination chip under a low denomination stack. If they win, they draw attention to it if it is missed. If they lose, it may go back into the dealer's chip tray with the other low denominations. The next thing is to spread to multiple hands of high stacks of the low denomination. With a win, the high denomination chip will probably be returned.

Over/Under 13

The over/under 13 is an interesting little side bet which can be very advantageous to the card counter. The sidebet is a simple affair. It is conducted independently of an ordinary game of blackjack. There are two spots in front of the player's regular betting circle, one marked "over" and one marked "under." A player may place a bet in either one of these circles. If he wins either bet he is paid off at even money. A score of 13 results in a loss for both bets and a win for the house. The over bet has a house expectation of over 6.7 percent while the under has an expectation of 10.1 percent, and therefore for the basic strategist are sucker bets to be avoided.

While the off-the-top expectation is staggering, the over/under game expectation shifts dramatically with the removal of the cards, much more dramatically than with regular blackjack. The average removal of a card per deck in regular blackjack results in a change of about 0.5 percent. By comparison, the removal of a card in the over/under game results in a four percent change in expectation, and, of course, favorable bets can be placed if the count goes in either direction. The huge house edge on the over/under only partially protects the house, and the card counter is still substantially better off than in the regular game.

There are a number of count systems for the over/under. By far the most popular and most widely used is the "Crush Count" which was first published by Jake Smallwood in *Blackjack Monthly* in March 1990, later becoming widely known from Stanford Wong's *Professional Blackjack* (Pi Yee Press). You simply count +2 for an Ace or a 2, +1 for a 3, and -1 for a 9 or any 10-valued card. Any true count of +3 indicates a favorable over wager, while any count under -3 indicates a favorable under wager.

The game can yield a 1.5 percent advantage with one of six decks cut out of play. The game is very sensitive to penetration, so do not play a game with two decks cut out of play.

This is because over/under bets do not occur very often, but when they do they can be very valuable.

Briefly, and for the first time, London was offering the best game in the world for over/under card counters. However, American teams of professional card players moved in on the casinos and burnt out the London game.

The game still exists, particularly in Eastern Europe, but because of the potential value of the sidebet when such a game does surface it is generally kept a secret.

My advice to the casinos is that they cannot be seriously hurt at the lower limit tables by card-counting over/under players, and that it would be wise to reintroduce it. It takes four times as many card counters as regular players to wipe out the casino advantage at over/under if they are all betting similar amounts.

Other Side Bets

You will see that various other side bets are sometimes offered at the blackjack tables such as "super 7s" and "royal match." These bets are not exploitable as a practical matter, so I will not discuss them except to say that they should be avoided.

How Professionals Affect Ordinary Players

Extensive literature exists on the mathematics and technical details of casino blackjack. Almost without exception the literature has been written with the intention of enabling members of the general public to become winning or, at least, more proficient players.

Consequently, all the writing on the subject takes the perspective of the individual player. However, the casino is *not* affected by an individual player's win rate, but by the effect of that player on the win rate of the *table*. This may come as a surprise to many casino executives, but the advantage player does not necessarily hurt the casino, and under certain circumstances may drastically *increase* the casino's hold! Blackjack has many of the features of a pari-mutuel game. It is not a game where investment is split among the players in a classic pari-mutuel game, but favorable cards are distributed in the same manner. *Blackjack is not a zero sum game where the casinos and player's interests are diametrically opposed.*

Take the following example: You are a pit boss whose sole aim is to maximize the win rate of your casino. You are watching a high roller flat bet the table maximum of $1000 on a four-deck game. You have been casing the deck and know there is an excess of high cards remaining. Suddenly a player jumps in and starts betting $100 a hand. You know this player is a professional backcounter—you have seen this man in the files kept by a detective agency that catches cheats and advantage players. What would you do?

If you answered "I would bar the player before he could make another bet," then you were incorrect, although I believe this is what 95 percent of casino executives would answer. In this instance, to bar the backcounter is to *lose money*. The backcounter is effectively shorting the deck of good cards. He, personally, is winning, but the high roller suffers because of the extra hands that have been taken away from him in a good deck. Because the high roller bets 10 times what the backcounter is wagering, the overall effect of the backcounter is to increase the win rate of the casino.

By how much? Over 100 hands the backcounter's win rate will be $20 (he is only playing a small number of these hands, though his advantage is quite large when he does play). Over 100 hands the high roller following basic strategy loses about $550. With the backcounter lurking about this rises to $650, an increase of $100. Overall the casino *gains* $80 per 100 hands because of the backcounter.

This phenomenon is linear with the number of decks, the casino always gains if the average bet of the backcounter is half that of the table, yet the effect is stronger the fewer the decks used.

If you add additional basic strategists the effect of the backcounter on the win rate of the table is the same; however, for each individual player the effect is diluted. If there were two high rollers in our above example each would lose $50 more per hour because of the good cards that were sacrificed.

Note that in actual play the backcounter is even more likely to benefit the casino. The above figures assume the counter plays perfectly. Clearly this is not possible. The mental drudge of playing like an automaton day after day leads to inevitable errors. In the words of Ken Uston, "An analogy might be made with tennis players—all players make mistakes: good players make very few." Therefore the expected win rate of the counter will be smaller than the above figure. By how much? Well, professional players regularly report that their actual earnings are no more than *one half* of their expected earnings.

Some card-counters do not vary the play of their hands with basic strategy, or use a limited range of indices. In this case their average expectation will be less. Also, the play of high-rollers, while generally above that of low stakes players, is generally worse than basic strategy. Certain errors are typical: they take insurance, they stand with stiff hands vs a 10 etc. These plays are erroneous with a full deck, yet they become correct when an excess of 10s remain. If the backcounter is taking cards away in these 10-rich situations then the effect of these bad plays is exacerbated.

Now, the perceptive casino executive might say, "But there are other considerations besides the raw amount of money won, I do not wish my high rollers game to be ruined by an undesirable player. I value their patronage more than the small extra gain produced for this comparatively short period of play." That is fair enough, except that I specified the case where the executive's sole aim was to maximize win rate. By all means, let casino operators use this information as they see fit, but they should at least be aware of it.

Note that the differences between the amounts being bet do not have to be nearly as drastic as in my example for the casino to benefit from the backcounter's intervention.

These figures suggest that if the backcounter's bets are large relative to the basic strategist he poses a noticeable threat to the casino. However, if the reverse is true the back-counter could save the casino a fortune!

Alternatively, it is possible for teams of advantage players to use the opposite tactic. A minimum bettor will sit at first base and spread to multiple hands in negative decks. A high roller will sit in third base and play basic strategy. The high roller's gains will far outweigh the Small Player's losses, yet neither exhibits play of the traditional card-counting variety. Only the sharpest of pit bosses will pick up on this.

Such a team can enhance their earnings further if the small bettors play their hands in order to "preserve" a high count or use up cards in a negative count for the benefit of the high roller. They can then appear to be playing very badly by making plays contrary to common sense when in fact they are boosting the win rate of the team. Of course, while most advantage players do not play every negative hand many do not fit into the strict backcounting variety either.

How does a more common variety of card counter affect the game? Well, it depends greatly on his style of play, not only how often he leaves negative decks but how many hands he plays in both positive and negative decks. The issue is complex: some card counters play several hands in nega-tive decks and play only one in positive situations. This style of play, known as "card eating," was pioneered by Ken Uston in *Million Dollar Blackjack*. It increases the expectation of the card counter by using up more cards in negative decks lead-ing to less money being wagered in those situations.

Conversely, many players do the exact opposite of this and play one hand in negative decks, spreading to multiple hands in positive decks. Why do they do this?

The reason is that although they play more hands in negative decks and slightly reduce their win rate, spreading to multiple hands reduces fluctuation. Fluctuation is greatest when the card counter has his large bets out, therefore spreading to multiple hands allows the card counter to lessen the wild streaks a full-time player must endure. Some players will also play multiple hands in order to exceed the table maximum.

The card eater has a beneficial effect on the expectations of each individual player at the same table. The player who spreads to multiple hands in positive decks has a negative effect. In both cases the effect on another individual player will not be as large as the advantage gained by the card counter, but the effect on the whole table may well be more significant than the expectation of the card counter, especially if more money is wagered by the players.

It may well be that card counters bet significantly less of their total bankroll than the average player because they fully understand the risks involved. The average players, by definition, do not understand the risk involved, which is certain and inevitable ruin if they play for long enough with a negative expectation.

The other well-documented method of blackjack advantage play involves analysis of the shuffle. The most well-known shuffle-tracking method involves cutting segments of unfavorable cards out of play. By itself this gets the shuffle tracker between 0.5–0.8 percent, and more importantly *so does everyone at the table*. This would seriously lead me to question the logic of the casino industry, which has slowly been abandoning single-deck games (which are easy to shuffle thoroughly and foil tracking) in favor of multiple-deck games (which are harder, and sometimes impossible to randomize without slowing down the game). Moreover the shuffle tracker wins at a much higher rate than the regular card counter. There is some compensation to the casino if the shuffle tracker does not play negative slugs. The shuffle tracker has a much better idea of when the deck is bad than a regular player, so this will ameliorate the effect of skilled cutting to a certain extent. The conclusions concerning spreading to multiple hands for card counters are also valid here, though even more so.

It should be recognized at this point by even the most obtuse casino executive that the full elimination of advantage players, even if it were possible, is not particularly desirable.

There is the potential for an effective compromise between advantage players and the casino industry whereby advantage players can exercise their skill without harassment and the casino can realize greater profits. For example, this can be achieved by permitting backcounters to play at the table minimum, or to a tenth of the table maximum as opposed to banning mid-shoe entries. Regular card counters could be *encouraged* to play multiple hands in positive counts. It is unlikely the advantage player will be making money for the house in each and every instance, but procedures should be considered so that the advantage player increases the hold percentage over the long haul. For example, a backcounter may enter a game with one other ordinary player betting $50. The backcounter may start betting $75. In this instance his presence is costing the house a small amount. Yet if there are high rollers betting $500 at three other tables in the casino, it is better to let the backcounter play this shoe, to prevent the likelihood of his moving into one of their games.

A final consideration is that the number of cards dealt can and should be increased when the advantage player is increasing the table win rate. For a long, long time paranoid casinos have been unnecessarily cutting large numbers of cards out of play to foil card counters. Card counters and some enlightened executives have argued this costs the casino far more in shuffle time and fewer hands per hour than it saves in the paltry losses to counters. Further, if an advantage player is increasing the table win rate, then dealing out more cards will also increase the win rate of the table dramatically.

Neutral observers might point out that such a cozy arrangement hurts the interests of ordinary players. However, this is not necessarily the case, since ordinary players are already paying for the huge cost casino surveillance and game protection measures, which would cease to be of such importance, and are already losing money to backcounters—whether the casino knows it or not.

It is possible that casino executives will dispute my contentions. By all means, casino operators should be critical of these findings: but *do your own research* and specify the particular game conditions to be offered. It is in your own interest to do this. But the general conclusions here cannot be contradicted. They are not assertions or opinions: they are fact. If you run simulations and your methodology is sound you will come to identical conclusions. Meanwhile, it is very likely that you're using procedures to save your casino money, that are actually costing your casino money!

Chapter 8
Blackjack and Sex
Revere's Challenge to
Female Players

Thirty years ago Lawrence Revere issued a challenge to all female blackjack players: "If you can count cards, you can win a million dollars at blackjack!" Revere simply did not believe that a woman could become a successful card counter, attributing this to feminine mystique clouding sound judgment. This might strike the reader in the new millennium as pure chauvinism, but Revere came from a much more traditional world, one where women rarely participated in mathematics or the sciences, so it is perhaps unfair to judge the great master too harshly.

But what of Revere's challenge? Has any woman won a million dollars playing blackjack? No. I have known, or heard of female blackjack players at the highest level, who have won as much as $100,000–$250,000. And certainly there have been many competent female players. It is possible that a female player may have been more successful and kept her talents hidden, but this is very unlikely. My contacts are very extensive and I do know personally—or know about—most of the big players in the world. Also, there are very few count players at the economic levels necessary to win a million dollars. I doubt such a player would escape the attention of blackjack's inner circle.

And that is a shame.

A card-counting female player has many advantages over her male counterpart. A woman will attract less attention because many pit bosses of the world share Revere's archaic view of their inherent abilities. Despite the seismic changes in the world outside, attitudes within the casino are closer to what they were 30 years ago. Las Vegas is a city without clocks in more senses than one.

A woman can spread her bets at least twice as much as a man and attract approximately half the attention. This is an incredible advantage.

Women players are not immune from barring. If the eye in the sky analyzes her play and discovers she is a counter, she will be asked to leave. However, it is much less likely that things will get to that stage.

Adversarial Betting

Two highly successful female blackjack players used an interesting method to hide their card counting skill. Recognizing that the pit pays women little attention, they would play at the same table and bet erratically in accordance with the count

Unbeknownst to the pit, however, they were averaging their bets to play in accordance with strict Kelly betting. For example, if the correct Kelly wager called for $25, one would bet $5, the other would bet $20. The next hand one would bet $15 the other would bet $5. Note that this has all the cover benefit while maintaining the advantages of correct betting. They were never caught, and are probably making money to this day.

Howie's Angels

Women have gone over to the dark side. Just as it can be unwise for a casino to underestimate the threat posed by a female counter, so can complacency by male counters when dealing with female surveillance agents.

According to Arnold Snyder (from the Spring 1998 issue of *Blackjack Forum*):

. . . I learned of another counter-espionage ploy being used in Las Vegas and Laughlin to identify professional blackjack teams. According to the late Paul Keen, my Las Vegas reporter at that time, ex–Uston teammate turned freelance counter catcher, Howard Grossman, had been training attractive women, who had become colloquially known as "Howie's Angels," to flirt with Big Players who were suspected of having team affiliations.

The angels would pick up players and get their details with the purpose of exposing team operations. Howard Grossman, who had a unique insight into the counter's mind, understood the counters had a "trophy" mentality towards women that became their Achilles' heel.

Influencing the Dealer

Renowned blackjack expert and Playboy model Missy Cleveland wrote in April 1979 of her trip to Las Vegas: "It's easy to double your money, just smile at the dealer." A smile from a female player can have the same effect as a tip. Ken Uston, in a throwaway line in *Million Dollar Blackjack*, remarked that his sister probably played with an advantage even though she was not a good player, as the dealer would tip her off to the likely value of a hole card. A throwaway line perhaps, but not a minor point, since just knowing when to take insurance gets a player two percent over basic strategy.

Uston further remarked that an attractive woman would not have much difficulty finding such a dealer.

Some dealers become so enamored of certain female players that they will shuffle on bad counts to help them win. I know of women who can induce this behavior in dealers with whom they are friendly and whom they tip occasionally. In single-deck games a dealer whose usual technique is to shuffle at the quarter-deck point on positive decks and half-deck otherwise, gives you 0.8 percent over basic strategy.

Enter Angie Marshall

Until recently there was no introductory text to blackjack written by a female author. This has changed with Angie Marshall's excellent *A Woman's Guide To Blackjack* (Lyle Stuart, 1999). Despite the title (it reminds me of those 1950s information films where women appear to have their brains sucked out through their ears) this is one of the best introductions to blackjack in print. Marshall presents a derivation of the Hi-Opt I system with a simplified playing strategy, which is an elegant combination of simplicity and power in hand-held games. Marshall explains the procedures and practice of blackjack with an admirable use of plain English. It makes fascinating reading, for the most part Marshall writes in airhead mode, then occasionally slips her cover whilst covering a technical point, and you see some of the inner woman come through. Marshall reports that she has never been barred.

Chapter 9
Buck Rogers Blackjack I
Machine vs. Counter

In the past few years a new countermeasure has emerged from the casino laboratories to foil blackjack card counters—the dreaded shuffling machine.

The premise behind the creation of such a device is simple; a machine can randomize a deck of cards more quickly and effectively than a human. Shuffle time is wasted time that could be spent dealing extra rounds. A round or two extra in an hour will make a staggering difference to a casino's annual profit margin. But casinos generally shuffle up with at least 25 percent of the cards remaining owing to the fear of card counters, who benefit greatly from seeing many cards dealt out.

The casinos must strike an effective balance between the two to optimize their profits. Except that the shuffle machines change all that, effectively they eliminate shuffle time. How this is achieved depends on the variety of shuffler. There are two distinct forms—the garden variety "autoshuffler" and the exotic "continuous shuffler."

The autoshuffler does away with "down time" by using two sets of cards, one set is being shuffled while the other is being dealt. Whenever the house wants a new shuffle it just inserts unshuffled cards into the machine and removes the freshly-shuffled pack.

The continuous shuffler is different. Cards are taken out of play and directly reinserted into the machine, usually before the round itself has been completed. There is no break in the action at all.

News of these machines created an almost hysterical response in the card-counting community. The implications were clear. Without a significant percentage of cards dealt out, card counting is ineffective. In the past the casinos were forced to deal out many cards because increased shuffle time would result in loss of action from ordinary players. Now they could eliminate shuffle time altogether, with the happy side-effect of making their games uncountable and unbeatable.

Except, it wasn't that simple.

The first generation of continuous shufflers were introduced at the Mirage in the late 1990s. Several teams of professional card counters burned out the game, making off with tens of thousands of dollars before the casino removed the machines.

How was this possible?

Cards That Do Not Reappear

There is a *latency of redistribution* in continuous shuffle machines. In layman's terms, this means cards played on one round probably won't appear on the next. Exactly when they will find their way back into the shuffle depends on the number of players, the speed of play, and most importantly the variety of machine itself. The exact figures can only be derived by peeking inside the machine or by statistical analysis.

Statistical analysis is no big secret, though very few card counters actually know how it works. Any statistics text book will tell you how to go about doing this. Basically you memorize a card on one round and look to see if it appears on the next. The chance of a card of any value being dealt is 1 in 52 with a single deck. The chance of it being dealt on the following round is 0 if it has not been redistributed into the pack. So if the card repeatedly fails to turn up on the following round, it is a very strong indication that the cards of the first round are not redistributed in time for the second round.

Now, most modern continuous shufflers use more than one deck. This brings up the problem of distinct cards. How on earth do we tell one Ace of spades from another? Surely this means we cannot work out the redistribution frequency?

In fact it is not that big a problem. We can use a simple method to determine whether or not cards are recycled immediately.

First, memorize the first three cards dealt on a round. On the next round, look at the first three cards (if you have good memory skills you can memorize more than three cards). Add 1 to a running total in your head if any of these three cards match the three cards you memorized from the previous round. You must play basic strategy and bet the table minimum while doing this.

Suppose four decks of 52 cards are being used. The chance of a match not occurring is 196/208 x 195/207 x 194/206 or roughly 83 percent. This assumes that the cards from the previous round have been redistributed into the shuffle. We can test this by calculating the standard deviation.

This is calculated by taking the number of hands—say, 1,000—multiplied by the probability of the first card being the first card of the subsequent round which is 17 percent, assuming a full shuffled deck. We multiply that by the probability the card won't appear again (83 percent). Finally we press the square root button on our calculator to get the standard deviation. The figure we get is 11.87.

The most likely outcome if cards from the previous round are redistributed immediately is that we will get 170 matches. We test for randomness by seeing if three standard deviations separates our actual from our projected results

(35.61). Therefore we have a fairly good idea that if the actual number of matches we get is less than 170 - 35 =135 then there is a >99.7 percent chance that the cards from previous rounds are not available for play. If the actual number of matches is between these two figures then more clocking is required for certainty.

Those 1000 hands played at $5 will cost the player $50, so this is not without cost. It will also require 10 hours of play. The best way to clock a shuffle machine is, of course, while not playing, but this is obviously impractical for very long periods.

The above figures are calculated on the basis of a hypothetical four-deck game with a player who memorizes three cards. You must alter the calculations if the conditions you are playing under are different, or you can easily memorize more cards per hand. Obviously the more you can memorize the fewer trials are needed.

In face-down games we can eliminate the need for a large number of trials. We can do this by exploiting the asymmetry of certain cards. If you look at the 6 of spades and turn it upside down you will see it is not symmetrical, i.e. it is recognizably different depending on which way you turn the card. Therefore, if you turn it one way, and turn every other 6 of spades the other way, then you will know when that particular 6 of spades has been re-dealt.

Once you have determined how many rounds it takes for cards to re-enter play, you can count on a round by round basis. For example if it takes three rounds for discards to re-enter play then you have to keep the count of the last three rounds in your head at all times. If the first three rounds you play are +2, -1 and +3, you now have a "total" count of +4. If on the next round you get a count of -3 then you rub out the first round count of +2, and now have a total count of -1, +3 and -3, which is -1.

Generally, it does not take that long for cards to return to play. This is not the same as counting a game with shallow penetration, since you are effectively playing the last hand of a game with shallow penetration, which is mathematically more attractive. This is why the Mirage machines proved so lucrative. The other advantage of playing a continuous shuffler is that there is no heat, because casino personnel think these machines are unbeatable. You will be able to obtain very large bet spreads with no attention.

I have heard rumors that new machines are under development which will virtually eliminate the latency of redistribution. Qualified sources have already told me there are machines in existence which will have a ready-to-deal stack only five cards short of the full pack. Would these machines be unbeatable? No. In fact they can be spectacularly profitable.

With these machines there is the possibility that cards taken out of play may return on the same round. If a player to my left is dealt the Jack of spades and busts, those cards will be returned to the discard tray and I may receive a Jack of spades as one of my hit cards on the same round.

It can be seen that a team can exploit this. A high roller could be stationed at third base. Small bettors can take up the rest of the table. The small bettors play in order to maximize the value of the high roller's hand.

For example, a high roller is dealt 16 against the dealer's six, and stands. A table minimum bettor to his left is also dealt two small cards. If the small player busts his hand those cards are returned into the continuous shuffler, which helps the dealer when he subsequently draws.

Dealers Who Forget to Reinsert Cards

Perhaps the auto-shuffler only shuffles after each round, thereby preventing the use of this strategy. What tends to happen then is that some dealers, not many certainly, perhaps one in 20, will forget to put back a handful of cards into the machine. Most of the time the dealer will reinsert the cards but leave a neglected handful of cards in the discard tray, which remain there deal after deal.

If these cards have a negative count (high in 10s and Aces), fine, point it out to the dealer and ask him to follow correct procedure. But if not, then you have an advantage on each and every hand! For example, say the cards have a +6 Hi-Lo count. If the machine uses three decks, then you will have a one percent edge on each hand. This is much better than a normal game of blackjack with a one percent edge, where you have the advantage perhaps only 10–25 percent of the time and have to make large bets when you do. With this game you can bet more aggressively. Also with this game you do not have to do anything but play basic strategy.

Autoshufflers: An Overview

Finally, what about the auto-shufflers used to make up shoes? Could a casino set these machines to say, 20 percent penetration and eliminate the threat of card counting? Currently, to the bemusement of card counters, tables with these machines are set to deal approximately the same percentage of cards as the human-shuffled tables. The reason for this is simple. These machines tear up the cards. The cost of replacing cards may eliminate much of the profits from low-limit tables. So, the casinos keep decks in play too long. There is so much card entropy, that the card backs become distinguishably warped if shuffling is frequent.

It takes visual acuity and a good memory to recognize the non-uniform characteristics of a card back, but it can be done if the cards are truly mangled. The gain from recognizing when an Ace is to be dealt as your first card is 2,000 times that of a card counter on each hand, assuming optimal bet-

ting. We are not talking about a minor edge. You could seriously threaten the casino's profitability in a short span of
time. In at least one instance, this type of coup has been successfully executed for over 100,000 dollars.

Theoretically, the casinos could use these machines at
the high-limit tables where the card cost is comparatively
unimportant. But high rollers are quite resistant to these
machines, as they are with any procedural change.

Consider, for example, the unnecessary ceremony of
baccarat, where typically 30 to 40 hands are dealt per hour.
On a mini-baccarat table as many as 600 hands could be dealt.
Yet, the casinos will not consider alienating their most valuable customers by replacing the big table game, despite the
fact that the decks of cards are discarded after each shoe
because they are so mangled by the players dealing them.

These machines were introduced primarily to cut
down on shuffle time. Shuffling cuts down drastically on a
casino's win rate. Time spent shuffling is time that could be
spent dealing another few rounds and increasing the hold
percentage. Shuffle machines can shuffle much faster than a
human, and eliminate much of the wasted time. Moreover
they can thoroughly randomize the cards, which is impossible for a human in any reasonable length of time. This elimi-
nates the threat of shuffle trackers.

For the basic strategist, the machines don't make much
difference, except that basic strategy players will lose more as
the pace of the game increases. For card counters the situation
is rather different. If the machine is of the standard variety, it
will simply replace the human dealer when a significant pro-
portion of the cards have been dealt out. This is a benefit to
the counter, since it allows him to play more hands per hour,
in fact it is a good idea to seek these machines out, all other
things being equal.

If the machine is of the "continuous" variety this creates problems. As each round is dealt the cards are inserted
straight back into the machine. When these machines first

appeared it was feared they would spell the death of card counting, since players thought they were playing against a deck which was shuffled up after every round. You couldn't vary your bets at all to take advantage of positive situations, because every round was dealt from a complete pack, or so it was thought. The gain from play variation in a single round, even from a single-deck, is small.

However, the prototype versions of the continuous shufflers, which were introduced in the Las Vegas Mirage casino, had a fatal flaw: cards that were put back into the machine were not immediately redistributed, some latency occurred. This meant players were not playing against a full deck of cards the whole time and the game could be counted like an ordinary game of blackjack. Moreover because there were always cards waiting to be dealt the game was played at a constant level of deep penetration. This was very lucrative for the professionals who discovered this. Using very large bet spreads they took the Mirage for several hundred thousand before the machines were removed.

The next generation of machines ironed out many of the problems. They contained a see-through front so that players could see what was going on inside and allay suspicions that they were being cheated. They utilized more decks so that they were not so vulnerable to card counters, and gave the house a larger advantage over the basic strategist. Also, by using more decks they were saving more shuffle time, since human dealers were pretty quick with one- and two-deck shuffles but are noticeably slower than a machine when shuffling many decks. The design was improved so that the cards did not "jam" so frequently.

However, attempts to introduce the machines into Las Vegas and Atlantic City failed. The players neither liked nor trusted them, and the dealers hated them as they felt they were being replaced. This fear is quite rational, the new machines have settings which can be adjusted at will and can be set to shuffle the cards in a completely predictable manner i.e. you would know exactly where each card went if you knew the initial order of the cards. This makes using a "cooler" (a stacked deck) or sequence very easy to put into play, in the same way a false shuffle (a shuffle where the cards stay in the same order but look like they have moved) would.

Despite this, in Europe, where paranoia of card counting is much greater, the machines have been quite common. In countries where card counters cannot be barred or have completely effective countermeasures taken against them, such as Holland, these machines have been universally adopted.

First, try and find out the number of decks in the machine, either by asking (this shouldn't arouse too much suspicion, it's a reasonable question) or by looking at the inside of the machine when it is being serviced or repaired.

Next, because these machines are all different, and are constantly being upgraded, you must "clock" how long it takes for cards to be redistributed. This means sitting down at the table, flat-betting the table minimum, and mentally recording the number of times cards repeat from one hand to the next, for 500–1,000 hands (the more the better) and determining the effective level of penetration. You will then know the level of penetration, which unlike a regular game will be at its deepest point on each and every hand.

Chapter 10
Optimal Betting
The Kelly System; Peter Griffin

How much you should bet and when you should bet it is an often covered and just as often misunderstood aspect of professional blackjack play. Most people read about proportional betting methodology and their eyes glaze over. If this theoretical stuff bores you, look more closely; the bottom line is that understanding how to bet proportionally to your capital makes a greater difference to the amount of hard cash you will earn from blackjack during your lifetime than anything else.

In the words of Arnold Snyder, editor of *Blackjack Forum*, "Most blackjack millionaires I know use Kelly betting." Kelly betting is the ideal compromise between acceptable risk and acceptable earnings. The term comes from J.L. Kelly's paper, "A new Interpretation of Information Rate" (*Bell System Technical Journal*). Kelly didn't actually invent his eponymous system, he just studied it thoroughly and understood its ramifications for gambling and investing. In investment circles Kelly betting is called "optimal geometric growth portfolio."

Kelly poses a hypothetical situation. What if a telegraph operator can delay the results of horse races to give himself enough time to go down to his local bookmakers and place a series of bets on foregone conclusions? How should he bet his money? Kelly's conclusion is that he should bet 100 percent of his capital, since the bet is a 100 percent certainty. After all, the gambler knows beforehand that it is going to win. Kelly expands on this example to derive his theory of optimal betting. A gambler should bet the percentage of his capital according to the *percentage advantage* he enjoys on any particular bet.

In theory this means the gambler should never (well, hardly ever!) be wiped out by a long losing streak. He will also win at a much faster rate than any other system of money management which does not contain an unacceptable risk of ruin. Risk of ruin just means getting your bankroll wiped out.

Kelly's is a relatively simple rule to apply if the payoffs are even and the gambler's advantage is constant. However, blackjack is a much more complex process. The correct Kelly bet is distorted, by double-downs, splits and insurance wagers, all of which increase the average bet size.

The average bet size of a player, factoring in the additional playing options, is 1.32 times the wager he actually places on the betting circle. So you divide your optimal bet by the ratio of a winning wager to a losing wager. With the Hi-Lo count each TC point is worth 0.52 percent, so a TC of +3 gets you a one percent advantage under British rules. You divide by 1.32 to give you the correct fraction of your bankroll to bet, which gives you three-quarters of a percent. So a player with $4,000 in the bank should bet $30 every time he has a TC of +3.

However while this betting scheme works well for Wongers, players who sit through some negative counts will find this method too aggressive, as the minimum bets they place will drain their capital. Under such circumstances the Kelly system would recommend not betting, or more correctly, making a negative wager. Obviously it's not possible to make a negative wager, and while it is occasionally possible to sit out a few hands, card counters do not generally do this as it draws unwanted attention. According to Edward O. Thorp, an effective compromise is to bet three-quarters of your capital, which works quite well with the four-deck game.

An intelligent simplification suggested by Stuart Perry, author of *Las Vegas Blackjack Diary* (RGE Publishing) is even more conservative, in line with Perry's experience of actual play, and he recommends betting half of your actual advantage and capping your maximum bet at one percent of your bankroll. The maximum bet is generally made at around the +4 true-count level with a level-1 system such as the Hi-Lo.

The disadvantages of a betting scheme like this are not as great as they might be. It's a surprising fact that betting half Kelly gives you 75 percent of the pure Kelly bankroll growth rate. And, in truth, most professional players find their actual edge is less than what they expected owing to a variety of external factors such as errors and lousy playing conditions.

Serious professionals use a bankroll equivalent to 150 of their "big" bets, which is their maximum bet when the count is sky-high. So if your biggest bet is $100, your bankroll should be $15,000. With such ratio, a bankroll will grow infinitely with only a negligible chance of being wiped out.

Players who play infrequently and recreationally may have little use for a Kelly system. The gains from the use of a Kelly system are not readily apparent during short sessions, and players may be unwilling to perform the calculations for the relatively small increase in return. But for the professional, it is absolutely essential that he uses Kelly. Protracted periods of play show spectacular gains for the Kelly bettor over the player who never adjusts his bets with fluctuations in his bankroll.

For example, who would win a million faster: two players starting with $100, one with a 10 percent edge just flat-betting $10, one with a one percent edge betting Kelly? The Kelly guy, huh? Maybe you sensed I was going to say that. What you probably didn't realize is that the Kelly guy will win *10 times faster*! You can see that the correct application of Kelly is much more important than anything else once the basics of card counting have been mastered. In theory, a Kelly counter, using a simple system, is going to win more than a player who marks cards but does not or cannot adjust his bet size upward to take advantage of a huge edge.

Perhaps you have a mental picture of the kind of wins and losses a card counter will experience. You may think of a series of wins punctuated by occasional losses, a slow and steady grind upwards. Nothing could be farther from the truth. A card counter experiences very violent swings in his capital and will often despair at long break-even or losing periods when he is playing perfectly. Many of your sessions will be decided by one hand, often involving doubling and/or splitting. Sometimes you will win a whole series of hands when the count says you are at a disadvantage, only to raise your bet when the count rises and lose back all your profit.

Fluctuation is the most serious difficulty facing the card counter. It places a strain on the player that many human minds are not equipped to bear. The euphoria resulting from big wins can also have very negative effects on the player's mental state. Note that the violent mood swings a card counter experiences are similar to clinical depression. For the four-deck player betting optimally and playing perfectly with a typical spread in a typical game, there is a greater than 25 percent chance that he will still be behind after 100 hours, or 10,000 hands of play. You do not only lose in negative counts. It is quite possible to lose over the course of several thousand of your maximum bets on positive counts. Frankly, if this doesn't drive you crazy, you were nuts to begin with! Even if they are winning, a significantly higher percentage of players will have only meager profits that will be scant recompense for their time. In fact, even these deflating figures understate the reality, since the bettor who resizes his bets will take longer to dig himself out of a long losing streak. You can also expect to lose half of your bankroll about a third of the time with perfect Kelly betting (which for various reasons is not possible to achieve in the real world).

Is there anything you can do about this? Yes.

Backcounting significantly reduces your chance of being behind. After 500 hours of backcounting only 1 in 50 players will be behind. This assumes playing TC's of +1 or more. A sensible strategy is to cut back on your bet size when half your bank is lost. This means you will "dig yourself out of the hole" slowly, but you have restored your risk of ruin to a reasonable level, and your total chance of ruin is small. Enduring fluctuation is the highest test of will and character for blackjack players.

It is a sad fact that professional players can expect little comfort from their friends or spouses during fallow periods, unless they are serious card players as well. Unfortunately the myth that you "can't win" has sunk deep into the popular psyche. If you are losing, most people will see you as a compulsive gambler. The fact that you have a "system" will not help, since all players say that. It is useless to try and educate people on this point. As long as you are not winning you have no credibility. For this reason it is best to communicate your losses, and for that matter your wins, on a need-to-know basis, or not at all.

Extra Edge: The Key to the Vault?

One rarely mentioned topic with regard to optimal betting is the relation between improvements in technique and lifetime earnings. Most players (with some justification), who learn that an additional set of indices gains them a mere 0.02 percent, or a side count gains them 0.05 percent, balk at the small return for the often considerable extra effort. But it's not quite that simple. Much more money can be made over long periods with a very small percentage increase in winnings than is readily apparent.

To explain why, you first have to do some little mental exercises, so that you are clear about the concepts involved. For example, take two players, A and B. Player A plays a game of coin tosses, winning every time heads comes up, and losing every times tails appears. Knowing that the coin is slightly biased towards heads Player A plays with a one percent advantage. Player B plays exactly the same coin game, only the coin he plays with favors heads twice as much, giving him a two percent advantage.

Both players bet according to the Kelly criterion. Each has $1,000 to begin with. How much will each have won after 100 hands? Well, Player A can expect to win $1,000, while Player B can expect to win $4,000. Player B wins four times as much money as Player A even though he is only winning twice as fast. This is because Player B's higher advantage means he is less likely to go broke and he can bet twice as much as Player A.

But Player B's advantage doesn't end there. If, at the end of 100 hands, the players decide to resize their betting levels in accordance with their bankrolls, which are now double their previous size, Player B can now bet $80, while Player A can only bet $20. In addition to his greater percentage win rate, and the larger amounts he can bet because of the lower risk, Player B now has a larger bankroll to bet from than Player A, and wins even faster than before. Previously, he was winning four times faster than Player A, now he wins eight times faster! Further, as the number of plays continues, Player B's bank will begin to dwarf Player A's and will, if they both play long enough, eventually become many billion times larger than Player A's.

Now, in blackjack, adding a side-count is not going to get you anywhere near a one percent advantage over the main system. Nor, in fact, will anything except mastering a very difficult method such as Ace location. But nonetheless, even quite marginal improvements in your win rate tend to increase your total winnings greatly over a long enough period.

To illustrate take two more players, one with a one percent advantage, one with a 1.05 percent advantage which is a rough approximation of two counters, one using a one-level system such as Hi-Lo, one using a multi-level system. The player with the one percent advantage takes 25 percent longer to double his bankroll six times (a realistic aim over the lifetime of a professional blackjack player). Therefore, for the serious player it always makes more sense to get as high a win rate as possible, and does lead me to question the advice of current authorities on the game who advocate simplicity above all else for the professional player.

Nevertheless, the best way to go about achieving a higher win rate is not always so obvious. New players often think that the best way to achieve a higher win rate is by moving to a higher-level system, learning more strategy indices or some other relatively minor improvement. Most advice in modern blackjack literature suggests that this increases the possibilities of mistakes. This is true, but simulation clearly shows that the effect of increased mistakes from moving to more complex methods of play is quite small unless the moves are unrealistically frequent.

However, there are other dangers associated with more complex play. You may be taking longer to play you hands, and five or six fewer hands in a hour will negate the gain from your improved techniques. You may spend longer practicing, time which could be spent actually playing and winning money. You may fail to notice dealer errors that go against you that you would otherwise notice. You may be less likely to detect cheating. You may be less able to carry off a convincing Act and end up getting barred or have to spread more aggressively.

It may be that the challenge of a complex system makes you more mentally alert, in which case by all means incorporate more skilled play. But look at some alternatives. Could you win more by trying to play faster? Most dealers deal at a speed largely determined by the players. Could you win more by learning how to bet your money more effectively? By playing fewer negative hands? By learning another method of blackjack advantage play? Or by spending more time scouting for better conditions? Only you can answer these questions. But any small improvement in play will carry great weight over extended periods of time though they might not be immediately noticeable in the short run.

Meet Peter Griffin

If you've never read anything by Peter Griffin but his name somehow sounds familiar, then you're in good company. Griffin published a seminal, brilliant and largely impenetrable work of genius *The Theory of Blackjack* (Huntington Press). Griffin was a mathematics professor who was stung by an initial encounter when trying out blackjack for the first time, and vowed revenge. After briefly considering chip forgery, he set his mind upon the task of investigating the mathematics of card counting. Despite his new-found expertise, and an initial period of success, he found himself cheated out of his bankroll (and collected enough evidence to prove it).

Confining himself to the role of theoretician, Griffin submerged himself in the arcane mathematical mysteries presented by the game. *The Theory of Blackjack* presents a picture of a humorous ("Griffin's winnings are rumored to run into the hundreds," went the cover blurb), modest and likable man, anything but the dry seriousness of the typical math nerd. But this belied Griffin's incredible voyage into the inner workings of an unseen world. Griffin went farther than anybody has, or is likely to go, in analyzing blackjack. He discovered methods of breaking down and analyzing the performance of various commercial counting systems, created a "perfect" count for almost every possible hand, solved decades-old conundrums such as the mysterious "floating advantage" and the effects of human error. In short, virtually everything of substance written on blackjack since Griffin's book has its basis in Griffin's work.

Despite its enormous influence, *Theory of Blackjack* is not a best-seller. This is partly because Griffin's work requires a high intellect and mathematical training to grasp, and is fully understood by virtually no one. Nevertheless, upon the sad occasion of his death in 1999, a New York Times obituary briefly catapulted his work into the spotlight.

It also emerged that Griffin, far from retiring from the game after initially being cheated at small-stakes play, had gone on to play for big money with some high-rolling professional teams. Did Griffin ever even the score? To tell the truth I don't know, but I like to think so.

Part III

The Future
and the
Fine Points of
Professional Play

Chapter 11
Blackjack Fallacies
Taking the Dealer's Bust Card; Crime; Cheating

Taking the Dealer's Bust Card

Ordinary players subscribe to many strange beliefs about how other players affect the run of the cards, most notably the belief in the third base player's controlling the dealer's cards. In general, however, players who do not count cards, or use some other advantage-play technique, do not affect other players at the same table in any way. Obviously, if third base draws a 10-valued card which would have busted the dealer had he not drawn, then that hurts the other players; but he is just as likely to have drawn a card which would otherwise give the dealer a winning or losing total, it all evens out for mathematical purposes in the long run.

The only way non-counting players can influence your edge is by making plays which increase or decrease the number of rounds remaining in the deck. For example, a player who splits 10s uses up a few extra cards when the deck is negative (ordinary players do not know the deck is negative, but if two 10s have just been dealt then it is more likely to be negative than positive). This may occasionally result in you playing a hand or two fewer than would be the case if you were alone. But this is a very minor effect of no real importance. It is amazing to think though that 10-splitters actually increase your expectation since the universal belief among ordinary players and dealers is that it does the exact opposite. You can sometimes clear a table by splitting 10s.

The Effect of Errors

In *Million-Dollar Blackjack* Ken Uston popularized the myth that one mistake an hour will cost you your edge. This is simply false. Simulation results show that the effects of making typical errors such as adding one to the true count, playing hands incorrectly, overbetting and so on are relatively minor provided they are not too frequent. Basic strategy gets you pretty close to even, and you can hardly do worse than basic strategy with a count system unless you do something unrealistically bad such as continually reversing the sign of the count. A more accurate perspective on the subject is given by Edward O. Thorp in *Beat the Dealer*: "It is an important and interesting fact that errors in card counting, if they are random, do comparatively little to harm the system player!"

Does the Shuffle Mess Up the Cards?

Some players believe that the casino shuffle orders the cards in a manner which puts the player at a huge disadvantage, as much as 10–20 percent. They state that card counting and basic strategy do not work because of the nonrandom shuffle and advise you to vary betting and playing decisions to take advantage of the shuffle. The methods of play based on these theories are generally referred to as "clumping" strategies.

There are a number of system-sellers peddling worthless systems based on this unsubstantiated principle. Prominent amongst these is Jerry Patterson, who was once a respected authority on blackjack before his involvement with the TARGET system, designed to exploit this nonexistent *non-random shuffle* phenomenon.

A number of card-counting experts, Bryce Carlson, Ken Fuchs, Stanford Wong, Mason Malmuth and Arnold Snyder have done extensive work on the effects of nonrandom shuffles. Did they conclude that the shuffle had no effect on player expectation? It may surprise you that they did not. But the effects were very small, no more than a few tenths of one percent; they were only noticeable under strange conditions where shuffling was very poor, and only after new decks were brought in, even then affecting players in each seat differently; and they were unaffected or *made worse* by the effects of using a nonrandom shuffle system such as TARGET.

Further, no shuffle produces exactly alike results. Even with the same house shuffle a different dealer will produce different results.

In conclusion, any effects of crude shuffling immediately after new decks are brought in will not significantly affect your expectation and are not systematically exploitable by the use of strategies designed to exploit clumping. Do not confuse card clumping strategies with methods such as shuffle tracking and Ace location. The latter methods have a sound scientific basis and their effectiveness can be verified empirically.

Can I Get My Legs Broken?

Not really. Forget any dreadful fantasies that might have been inspired by the film *Casino*. The enhanced power of the various gaming bodies has been largely successful in eliminating organized crime from casino gambling. Today's casinos are generally run by large leisure or hotel chains with established reputations. They are not criminals, at least officially, nor would they willingly employ mobsters.

Card counters of the past have suffered harassment and did very occasionally endure physical violence. The techniques you will be using as a card counter are entirely legal. That would place any modern casino that chose to injure any player physically in a very insecure position in these litigation-happy times. It is difficult to see what a casino could gain from physical abuse of a player except very bad publicity and a huge damage payout, not to mention the loss of its license.

Harassment of a generally legal, but not much more pleasant kind, does exist however. The danger, if any, comes from the Griffin detective agency, (no connection with Peter Griffin, the writer and theorist), an organization devoted to catching cheats and advantage players. It keeps a book on individuals noted as "threats" to its casino subscribers and makes no distinction between those who are gaining their edges legally and those who are not. It becomes very difficult to enter a casino once you are in the book. Griffin typically juices up the activities of individuals in the book by claiming, for example, that a regular card counter is a computer user, or that a shuffle tracker is suspected of marking cards, etc. A number of people with affiliations to known advantage players are included in the book, their only crime appears to be breathing the same air as their card counting acquaintances.

The Griffin organization monitors its member casinos by remote VCR and will instantly identify a threat and notify the casino. Here is part of an advertisement for them:

The Griffin 2000 system as developed to bring the expertise of Griffin Investigations to your casino within minutes of the discovery of a potential problem. While your personnel evaluates the play, the Griffin 2000 system transmits images of the players involved to Griffin Investigations where our investigators will review the pictures at any time of the day or night. The pictures are transmitted by telephone, and are the same clarity and resolution as the images on your surveillance monitors.

Griffin will, of course, follow and harass advantage players by more traditional private investigation methods. The card expert and author of *Blackjack Bootcamp*, Allan Pell, actually recommends learning MOSSAD anti-detection methods in order to deal with Griffin.

The Effect of High Counts

Another common fallacy among blackjack players is that very high counts win less than moderately high counts. For counts such as the Hi-Lo, which count the Ace the same as a 10, there is no truth to this at all. There is no point at which a high count becomes disadvantageous.

For Ace-neutral counts such as Hi-Opt or the Zen Count, there is a theoretical point at which advantage reaches a peak and then begins to deteriorate. (To take the extreme case, if the deck is composed solely of 10s, every hand will be a push.) But reaching the point where the count is so high that the advantage begins to deteriorate is an event which is unlikely ever to occur in any game except single deck. Even if it did, this is of no real importance to a player's betting strategy. In the above example, it does not matter that the player has a maximum bet in front of him, since he cannot lose either. And in any case the count will only get that high once every few ice ages, at least in a shoe game.

With an Ace-reckoned system your advantage will never decline to any degree. A deck full of Aces and 10s has a 68 percent edge which you would be foolish to pass up. Since mildly and extremely positive counts both have very high advantages, it is inconceivable that advantage declines at some intermediary stage.

Will I Get Cheated?

A casino is unlikely to systematically cheat players. The casino has, in the house edge, a license to print money, it does not need to cheat. Of course, human greed sometimes overcomes rational considerations, and there may also be some dealers cheating for themselves.

Nevertheless, it is always advisable to be on your guard. A persistently nefarious individual can find a way to part you from your money. A dealer could interlace the cards in certain unfavorable sequences, pay you off short, or strip the deck of a few 10s or an Ace. For this reason, always be reasonably cautious if a.) the shuffle causes certain cards to stay undisturbed, b.) you are persistently paid less than you bet, or c.) the deck always seems to be a couple of 10s or Aces short. Probably this is nothing more than chance. But if you are persistently losing, it is perhaps better to seek a game elsewhere to be safe.

Does My Doubling-Up System Work?

No! The fact that virtually every gambling book ever written denounces this system as worthless, does not stop a new generation of players from discovering this system for themselves. Doubling-up is known as the "martingale" system. It involves doubling your bet each time you lose, and going back to the table minimum every time you win, so the sequence would be (assuming a $25 minimum) $25, $50, $100, $200, and so on. The theory is that you will never experience a number of losses in a row that will take you up to the table maximum. It should be apparent that in the above example six straight losses will take you over the table maximum in a

Vegas $1,000 game. Even with a much larger table maximum you will hit the limits soon enough. Advocates of the martingale system argue: "Can I lose eight, 10, 15 times in a row?" The answer is a resounding, "Yes!" There is no theoretical maximum to the number of times you can lose in a row. Of course, the higher the number of consecutive losses the less likely it is to occur, so a player with a large bankroll could grind ahead with small profits for a while. But to have a good chance of avoiding total wipe-out he must only win a small amount in relation to his bankroll. Effectively you are trading a greater chance of a large loss for a better chance of a small win. These balance each other out perfectly, because the martingale does nothing to change the house edge. Use it and ruin is certain, inevitable, and final.

So, can any progressive system beat the house? We'll see.

Chapter 12

A Progressive Betting System That Actually Works!

Progressive betting systems are one of the most controversial subjects in gambling and particularly in blackjack. Naturally as a player who believes in the math, I am going to come down on the side of . . . well, dammit, I am going to come down on my own side, because I am not really happy with the argument of either camp.

More hysteria and misinformation about the subject of progression betting has been written than has been written about any other gambling subject. Gamblers with an intellectual interest in gambling fall into two basic categories. There are players who follow scientific methods, based on mathematical models and computer simulation. The second category involves gamblers who use scientifically unproven methods, or their intuition. There is often a rational basis for these ideas, and they may involve pseudo-scientific concepts but their justification depends on argument rather than data.

The biggest class forming this latter category use progression systems. I get at least one e-mail a week from the user of some form of progression system. Generally, I do not comment on such methods, except to point such individuals in the direction of works by Thorp, Epstein, and Levinson which prove the futility of using betting systems to overcome a negative expectation. Basically I know before I have been informed of the details that the system, particularly if it is being peddled by some charlatan with promises of easy wealth, is worthless. This goes not only for blackjack but for all forms of gambling, regardless of the particular system.

However, the game of single-deck blackjack is a minor exception to the general rule. There is a small but tangible correlation between advantage and the results of the previous hands before the last shuffle.

The effects, calculated by John Gwynn and published in a 1986 edition of *Blackjack Forum*, revealed that:

1. Following a win, player advantage decreases by 0.10 percent.

2. Following a loss, player advantage increases by 0.12 percent

3. Following a push, player advantage decreases by 0.15 percent

This phenomenon tends to embarrass blackjack experts because technically it makes the old argument that "progression systems do not change the house edge" incorrect. Unfortunately, the popular progression systems do not exploit the win/loss correlation properly. None of the popular systems increases expectation by more than 0.05 percent even in single-deck games. The reasons for this are several:

1. The effects of the win/loss correlation are quite small. The effects are far weaker than even the simplest counting systems.

2. They do not take into consideration the number of unplayed cards remaining.

3. Crucially, the progression is not reset at the shuffle.

4. Wins at the minimum bet are ignored.

It is technically possible to design a progressive system that can win at blackjack, but in practice the gain would be so small that it would hardly be worth pursuing.

John Gwynn tried to design such a system. In the *Theory of Blackjack*, Peter Griffin reports briefly on the results of Gwynn's extensive simulations which showed a win/loss correlation between hands equivalent to 0.2 Hi-Lo points (0.1 percent off the top of the deck). The reason is simple; winning hands are somewhat more likely to contain high cards, resulting in a depression of advantage and vice versa.

Leon Dubey expanded on Gwynn's ideas in his *No Need to Count* (1981), which includes a number of other "situational" effects, such as the increase in advantage following hard double-downs and non–Ace pair splits. Commenting on Dubey's system in his *Blackjack Wisdom* (RGE Publishing), Arnold Snyder stated that even in the most favorable single-deck games, Dubey's system might win a dollar or two per hour if the player were to spread his bets from $1–$20. Snyder was writing for an audience that knew there would be horrible and frequent losing sessions associated with the use of such a system. Snyder mentions that such wild bet variation would frequently get the player barred, as apparently happened to Dubey.

Nevertheless, there are perhaps a few angles that have not been exploited. If you were to try to create a winning progression system, here are some ideas which may help:

1. Find a single-deck game with rules that give you a break-even edge off the top with basic strategy.

2. Look for games that deal out a great deal of cards, 75 percent is excellent. You must play alone with the dealer or the system will not work.

3. Keep a count of wins and losses, for the deck you are playing only, i.e. only count wins and losses since the shuffle. Have one pile of chips record wins, another losses, another pushes. Simply add a chip to the relevant pile each hand.

4. Leave the table after three successive losses or pushes. You are at a large disadvantage now. Ideally you

would leave the table every time there were more wins and pushes than losses, but you would end up leaving the table so often this would be impractical.

5. You can change your playing strategy with knowledge about wins and losses. Stand 16 vs. 10 when losses outnumber pushes and wins. Also hit 13 vs. 2 and 12 vs. 4.

There are other simple ideas you could add based on "situational" information. You could leave the table after an Ace-split, for example. But there are dangers to adding too much information to a system whose chief value is its simplicity.

This system will reduce the house edge to a mild extent, and also reduce your overall losses, since your total action will be smaller. But then the very simplest count such as Ace-5 will do better. Progressions would have been more effective in the pre–World War II days of single-deck blackjack dealt down to the last card. It is even possible that the systems may have given some pre-war players a small advantage over the casinos, since the effects of the wins and losses with all the cards dealt out are much stronger. It is also interesting to note that players who use a martingale system in hand-held games will be making maximum bets in what on average will be a positive count. Do these players get barred, or mistaken for card counters? How much have casinos lost by confusing the two classes of players?

In anything other than a single-deck game where many cards are dealt out the effect is comparable to the gravitational effect of a butterfly's wings on the moons of Saturn. Progressive systems are not going to make you a millionaire. They may give you a little entertainment, if that is how you like to play. But they do also have useful mathematical properties which are worthy of discussion.

A word to the unwise: if you ignore all the warnings, choose to ignore the accumulated wisdom of decades of blackjack knowledge, and selectively interpret the revelations of this chapter, you deserve what you get, which will be swift and inevitable financial annihilation. Challenge the broad and fallow plains of infinity at your peril. Many have traveled there. None have prospered.

Getting an Edge in Single Deck

It is the opinion of most modern professionals that the slowly-vanishing single-deck game is inferior to the shoe game when it comes to the practical business of winning money at blackjack. While single-deck is mathematically superior to the multiple-deck game, for ordinary players and especially card counters, the game is closely watched by pit personnel, making it difficult to win money consistently without frequent barrings. Modern professionals face two choices, play shoe games or try something other than traditional card counting.

Personally, I hate playing shoes, though I am often forced to by geography. The game is simply much less interesting than single deck. Nothing makes much difference to your edge except shoving more money out; the subtleties of single deck are far more exciting.

Nevertheless, it is still possible to win consistently at single-deck without being frequently barred, and there are approaches which give you an acceptable win rate. The simplest approach is to flat bet the single-deck game. Few casino personnel are capable of detecting a counter through play of the hands alone. However, this is only worthwhile under special conditions; you need a break-even game off the top, deep penetration and a count system optimized for playing efficiency to gain a one percent edge.

Several advanced methods of gaining an edge have been outlined in *Blackbelt in Blackjack* by Arnold Snyder (RGE Publishing). Snyder explains the concepts of "opposition betting" and "depth-charging." The first method involves betting randomly throughout the shoe but averaging higher amounts in positive counts. The second involves raising your bet in increments as the cards are dealt out regardless of the count, to capitalize on the increasing gains from playing strategy as more and more cards are seen.

Two methods I have used can be effective. The first involves one player betting three hands at table minimum while another places a large wager on the fourth hand. In positive counts you play only the one hand. This has two benefits, you are "eating cards" in negative decks, and your losses in negative decks are the lesser because your playing decisions on your main wager benefit from having seen the other hands played out.

When I suggested this idea on the bj21 Internet newsgroup, Norm Wattenberger, author of the excellent *Casino Verite* responded with these comments:

After trying several different configurations, I ran 600 million rounds with two players as follows:

Rules: DD, DOA, DAS, No resplit, 75 percent penetration.

Player 1: Hi-Lo with perfect TC calculation. Always bets $15 as follows

TCTC 0, 1: two hands

TC>1: one hand

Player 2: AO II no side count, always bets $250.

Results: Player 1 lost $11.24/hour and Player 2 won $79.92/hour for a total of +$68.68. This is an overall advantage of 0.252 percent.

However, this methodology is ultra-sensitive to penetration. I reduced penetration by a mere four cards and lost half of my advantage. I increased it by six cards and gained about 28 percent. I created a chart of advantage by hand depth. This chart shows a far steeper incline than is normal. It is not at all surprising that the incline is greater. But, in my mind, the criticality of penetration makes this game too risky unless you are positive that the penetration is acceptable.

Also obviously, if Player 1 can bet table minimum advantage improves. (You save $7.50/hour.) I have many times seen casinos waive the rule that playing multiple hands requires a multiple of table minimum. However, I would expect that you would have difficulty having this rule waived when there is a much bigger player at the same table.

This technique can be improved with intelligent play of the small bet hands. Because their outcome is of little or no importance to you, you can misplay the hands in order to further eat cards. It is advisable for example to split 10s so that you may play one less big hand before the shuffle. Your play seems crazy to the pit, since you are departing from basic strategy by "engineering" the deck in your favor. Ideally, because the play is so unusual, you would have a partner play the small hands. This would avoid them barring you because "they figured you must be doing something." I doubt there is a pit boss in Nevada or New Jersey who could detect a partnership using this technique correctly.

Note that Wattenberger requires the Big Player to use a level-2 system, the Advanced Omega II count. The Hi-Lo, a good betting system but poor at playing the hands, would underperform by several tenths of a percent if also used by the Big Player, so the high roller would need to spread his bets to obtain a worthwhile advantage.

There is a variation on this strategy whereby the small bettor will spread to multiple hands off the top and cut back to one deep in the deck. The idea is to maximize the number of hands the BP will play deep in the deck, where the gains from bet and play variation are greatest. This is a viable winning strategy on its own and will minimize the house edge.

Progressive Depth Charging

Another method involves using a progressive betting system, in conjunction with a count system optimized for playing efficiency such as AOII. The crucial condition is that you must reset your bet at the shuffle. There is a weak correlation between the loss of a hand and increased advantage (about 0.1 percent or 0.2 Hi-Lo points), so you gain a little from betting more after a loss. There is also a mild depth-charging effect, since you always start with a minimum bet and can only increase it by following the progression as more and more hands are dealt out.

I was first enamored with the possibilities of using the most popular of betting systems, the Martingale. Because it is such a well-known method it is virtually perfect cover. I simulated a heads-up SD game with Reno rules and 75 percent penetration. I then tested the results of a flat bettor and a Martingaler spreading from 1–64 units in accordance with a strict progression, the one exception being that the bet was reset at the shuffle. Both players used AOII. The Martingaler outperformed the flat bettor by 0.4 percent, a noticeable improvement. However, I had been warned by leading experts of the dangers of increased fluctuation from the use of a progressive system. Sure enough, when I looked at the increased risk it was quite high enough to require a larger bankroll for the same risk of going broke. Simply, any gain would be canceled out by increased risk. Nevertheless, this method may have some utility for players who, for whatever reason, have a bankroll in excess of that necessary for the table limits at which they choose to play. They will never get barred using this approach.

There is another well-known and easily recognizable system: the D'alembert or pyramid progression, the Martingale's less volatile cousin. You cannot gain all that much from this, between 0.15 percent and 0.30 percent over flat betting, depending on the penetration, the rules and the progression you are using. However, I have found this approach is also much more effective cover than flat-betting. Systems such as the Fibonacci or the Labouchere are ideal as they escalate rapidly but retreat after a series of wins. However, these may not be easily recognized by the pit as progressions.

In conclusion, progressive systems contribute something to your edge. The less volatile systems will subtly increase your profits and any progression will increase your percent advantage. They are superior to flat-betting. However, they are not a substitute for raising your bets in accordance with the count.

Chapter 13
Buck Rogers Blackjack II
Machine vs. Dealer

New students of blackjack are often fascinated by the idea of designing a computer to play blackjack perfectly. Casinos go to extraordinary lengths to prevent the use of such devices at blackjack play, and have succeeded in getting laws passed making such devices illegal. Whenever blackjack is discussed in journals or computer discussion groups, a popular topic of conversation is how to go about making, or buying, such a machine, and how much advantage this will give you.

The idea goes back to 1963 when Robert Bamford of the Jet Propulsion Laboratory, designed an electric analog device to provide an approximation of the best strategy for a given deck subset. Unfortunately, Bamford was unable to persuade the casinos to take his machine on. However, that same year three Los Angeleans persuaded the Tropicana Hotel to accept a match from their bulky LGP-21 computer. In a one-hour match, witnessed by Thorp himself, the machine won $360, which was fifty times its average bet.

However, these machines were too bulky, and unreliable, for the stealth and subterfuge necessary for the professional counter. More than a decade passed before sufficient miniaturization made a concealable computer possible.

At this point, Ken Uston enters the story. Uston was one of the most successful blackjack practitioners of the 1970s and 80s, renowned for organizing team raids reputed to have taken several million dollars from the casinos. Uston explains in his extraordinary work *Million Dollar Blackjack* (Carol Publishing) how he became involved with silicon blackjack:

In January 1977, a fellow I'll call Jerry H. phoned me at the jockey club in Las Vegas and said that he could play perfect blackjack in a casino, far beyond the capability of the human mind—or for that matter, a dozen human minds.

Uston went on to recount the tale of how the computer was developed, a primitive prototype piece of technology, developed in a Frankenstein's laboratory of solenoids, soldering guns and electronic components. Designed to operate in a set of "magic shoes" operated by toe, the machine was a world away from today's all-powerful user-friendly CPUs. It communicated in the computers own binary language and took a month's training to be operated by a skilled player. It was vulnerable to a myriad of technological problems.

The team that was going to use this device was operating in a Las Vegas rather more hostile and less hospitable than today. The team took no chances; the machines were built to self-destruct on investigation. The computers were christened "David" but bizarrely, or maybe as an indication of the heat and paranoia going down, Uston gave them the alias "George" when writing about them in his *Million Dollar Blackjack*.

Uston operated the machine in casino conditions with initial success, but his winnings were eaten up by expenses. Returning refreshed from a brief European sojourn, Uston assembled a team of high rollers and went to battle Las Vegas, playing with the full power of a high-rolling team bankroll and perfect play. They cleared $130,000 before they saw the familiar sinister visages of known Griffin agents beginning to tail them.

Sensing the heat, the team split for the scenic beauty of Lake Tahoe. They continued to win, but a human failing brought about the team's downfall. The players were betting $1,000 a hand, which was not unusual in Vegas, but highly irregular in Tahoe. The casino personnel had a good information network and worked out that there was something amiss. They arrested several of the team members and confiscated one of the Davids, apparently suspecting it of being an electronic bomb.

As these stories passed into legend, a new generation of counters purchased bootleg versions of "David" called "Casey," and set off into the darkness with their algorithms blazing . . . and lost their shirts.

Most people read to the end of Uston's chapter in *Million Dollar Blackjack*. A less well-known article in *The Gambling Times Guide To Blackjack* (Carol Publishing) reveals the sequel to the story. Uston briefly recounts how successive teams found it impossible to operate the computers successfully under casino conditions. The complexity involved in mastering the binary toe inputs essential to conveying the value of each card to the computer and decoding its signals was simply beyond human capability at that time.

There was, and is, a great deal of confusion surrounding the power of computer blackjack play. These ideas spring from misconceptions concerning blackjack theory and the limitations of computers. The card-counting systems designed for humans, when used correctly, approximate computer-perfect play to a very high degree of accuracy. Professional players can determine when to raise their wagers almost perfectly—there is virtually no room for improvement.

Computers can play their hands better than their human counterparts, but this is not where most of the card counter's profit comes from, at least in the six decks which are currently the norm. The bottom line is that a six-deck player spreading from 1 to 12 units gains about 0.1 percent using a computer over the gain from a one-level commercial system such as Hi-Lo. You have to go to the very best Reno games with deep penetration before the gain becomes more significant, where the computer will outperform the human by 25 percent, owing to the increased importance of playing variations. This is assuming you can operate the device successfully (use of a computer greatly increases error) without ending up in jail. And such things don't come cheap, even if you build it yourself.

Most people greatly overestimate the power of such machines because the literature on the subject has become outdated. In the single-deck games dealt down to the last card, a computer can indeed outperform a human player. It can figure out the last card to be dealt by deduction for example, and work out a perfect strategy for that play. But such games don't exist anymore. With a shoe game where more than a deck is cut out of play the computer will rarely make a different decision from that of a competent counter.

You might think that a computer playing perfectly would play in a vastly superior manner to a human. But, computers don't play perfectly either. To do that, they would have to calculate the probability of each possible combination of cards occurring for every partially depleted deck encountered. Even for a computer this is almost impossible for large subsets of cards. Computers make approximations too, just better ones than their human counterparts. With the Nevada and Atlantic City courts ruling the use of a computers illegal, the game is really up for the silicon card counters.

Or is it?

Well, there are places in the world where the use of a computer is not necessarily illegal, or the subject is in a gray legal area. And there is one crucial development in blackjack which has been incorporated into the latest generation of magic shoes.

In Bryce Carlson's *Blackjack for Blood*, he reveals how he came across a computer called Black Magic designed by a group of card hustlers. It had been programmed to analyze human riffling and could predict the dealers hole card on each and every hand with a very high degree of accuracy. Naturally this would allow the player to win money at a staggering rate. Knowing the hole card 75 percent of the time, as the machine Carlson describes did, would get a three to four percent edge for the player.

It is a fairly short step to a set of magic shoes which could predict the first card of each hand and could predict hit cards, using much more complicated methods than those available to a human. Richard Epstein estimated in his *Theory of Gambling and Statistical Logic* (Academic Press) that a 40 percent advantage would be obtainable with perfect prediction based on the shuffle. Fortunately for the gambling industry, I do not believe such a device has yet been created. But, given the nature of human endeavor, it is only a matter of time.

Chapter 14
Miscellany
Preferential Shuffle; Hole-Card Play; Card Readers, etc

Advanced Betting and Play

Most of the gain (usually 80 percent or more) from card counting comes from betting. It is strange then that most attempts to improve upon existing commercial systems have concentrated solely on playing. Most theorists seem to think that because most responsible systems have very close to 100 percent betting correlation, that they cannot be improved further. This is not true, since the "model" betting correlation is based on is not *perfect* betting, just a very good *approximation* of perfect betting.

One of the areas where the commercial systems break down is with extreme end-deck subsets because they are designed to cope with mild deficiencies or excesses of cards of a particular rank in an otherwise standard deck. This assumption can be wildly inaccurate at deep penetration. The structure of the deck can break down creating a different set of effects.

For example, when Aces no longer remain in a deck, most systems will tell you that you are at a disadvantage. What no system will tell you is that even if a lot of 10s remain, the value of the 10s themselves is less (only 25 percent of that with a full deck) because they are not so important now that they cannot be paired with Aces and give you a three-to-two blackjack. Consequently if you factor this into your betting you will be outperforming the best existing commercial betting systems.

Interestingly, with no 10s left in the deck you have an advantage of 1.62 percent if you know the best strategy. Unfortunately this will hardly ever occur. Many was the time I thought of trying to sell this proposition to a casino as an ingenious double-bluff. ("Hi, Mr. Trump? I am trying to prove that card counting is a myth designed by the casinos. I want to challenge you to a million dollar freeze out, and I want you to take all the 10s out of the deck. My brilliant doubling-up system will take you to the cleaners.") Further, other weird subsets of cards can also give the player large advantages. If 10s and 9s are removed from the deck the edge is 10 percent, while also removing the 8s doubles the player edge.

The Preferential Shuffle

Preferential shuffling is the inverse of card counting. It involves the dealer keeping a card count and shuffling up on positive counts, thereby reducing the effectiveness of card counting and causing all players at the table of whatever skill level to lose faster. It is a tactic that somehow remains legal owing to the power of the casinos over the judicial system. In my opinion, it is cheating pure and simple. It is mathematically equivalent to stripping a deck of 10s and Aces.

Most casinos do not use the tactic. There are enough players savvy enough to recognize it and warn others, so it is usually a bad financial decision. It tends to be practiced by smaller venues. It is thought, generally, that preferential shuffling makes a game unbeatable. That is not always true, it depends on the extent of the shuffling. John Imming, writing for the Usenet *rec.gambling.blackjack* forum provided simulation data of a single-deck downtown Vegas game (double down on any two cards, dealer hits soft 17). It took a game where a dealer dealt down to one-half a deck when the deck was favorable, and a one-fourth deck when unfavorable. A player spreading his bets from one to four won at the rate of 0.65 percent. This is less than half what the same player would win if the dealer simply dealt down to 20 cards each time. But the player was still winning.

Just to remind the reader that the dealer's motivation may not always run in the same grooves, I have already suggested one potential area for player—favorable shuffling in my chapter on women players. In shoes, quite mild preferential shuffling puts the game beyond the reach of the most skilled and daring of counters, knocking 0.5 percent off your *off-the-top* basic strategy edge when shuffling is employed at any +2 count.

For the card counter it is not really a problem, as a count-based strategy is easily detected by any other count system. The card counter should just leave the casino. Ordinary players have no idea what's going on. For such players the only clues will be wide variation in the shuffle point and a minor delay in the dealers pick-up action indicating he is studying the cards.

Team Play and the Big Player

In the 1970s large numbers of card counters got together to take literally millions from the casinos of Las Vegas and Atlantic City with a concept known as the "Big Player." Counters would sit down at the table and flat bet while mentally recording the count. When it became noticeably positive they would give a surreptitious signal to one or more individuals who would sit down at their table and flat bet the table maximum. In this way the team was able to get effective spreads of 50-1 or more. Naturally their advantage was huge.

The legendary Ken Uston's team made several million dollars with this technique. Unfortunately, while teams still exist today, the method has become largely unworkable as it has become well known among casino personnel. Uston's book, *Million Dollar Blackjack*, details the procedures used by his team and these have now become common knowledge.

This approach is often impractical because the paucity of high-limit tables, the fewer number of tables in each casino, the infrequency of high true counts, and the rarity of high-stakes bettors, make such play highly conspicuous. With the exception of some Asian players who flit from table to table, this style of play is atypical of high rollers, who prefer marathon sessions at the same table.

In any case, the psychology of modern team play is different now than it was in Uston's day. Uston reported that thefts from the team bank were rare, rare enough not to pose a serious threat to the financial viability of such a venture. I believe this was the case in the games in which his teams played, but they operated in very favorable conditions where long losing streaks were rare. Had the teams expected win rate been lower, and their fluctuations greater, as a modern team would experience, the temptation for players to rip off the team, or to suspect others were doing so, would have been greater. To my mind this makes such a venture unattractive; the mathematics of blackjack I understand and trust; human nature I understand and do not trust.

Variations of the team approach may still prove workable. Uston's team invented a concept known as the Gorilla BP. This involved using a high-rolling player, already well known to the casino as a loser, making his playing and betting decisions on the signal of an expert player located on the periphery of his field and vision. The Gorilla BP does not even have to look at his cards to know the correct decision, and can put on as much of an Act as he wants without detracting from his standard of play.

More recently shuffle trackers have exploited the BP concept. The BP is called in only at the top of the shoe when a small bettor at the same table has cut a 10-rich card slug to the top. Thus the BP makes his big bets off the top of the shoe, leaving when the slug is exhausted, or continuing to play with his own knowledge of the count, plus any information his shuffle-tracking partner gives him on the remainder of the shoe. Shuffle trackers may also play at the same table to relieve the mental burden of shuffle tracking and to combine various methods. For example, one player may concentrate on cutting the cards favorably, another may sequence the Aces, another may look for rich segments, another may use a conventional card count.

However, the most traditional, least interesting, and still the most effective method remains for players on a team to play separately.

If you have a $5,000 bankroll (about the minimum for a shoe player who wants to play professionally) you will never bet more than $50 if you want to maintain an acceptable level of risk. If you play with another partner who uses the same scheme, plays in the same games, and plays as well as you, then you will experience only 70 percent of the fluctuation that a lone counter would. Since fluctuation is arguably the worst element of professional blackjack, this is very desirable.

Alternatively, you could try to win more money but remain with the same chance of bankroll wipeout. Simply, if your partner brings another $5,000 to the game, then you could both bet up to $100. If you find another four players, and each of them brings $5,000 to the team bank, you could bet $250 and so on. All other things being equal, this is a very good arrangement.

One method typically worked by modern teams is for a backcounter, or backcounters, to act as a spotter for a Big Player. This requires the spotter to backcount and signal the Big Player in to a positive shoe. With a number of spotters, any table in the casino that goes positive can be detected. This is mathematically very advantageous as it cuts out the dead time associated with backcounting. This approach has the notable advantage that spotters are often new card counters with no bankroll to invest, who can be paid a fixed wage. The Big Player wins at a faster rate and his bankroll is never touched by the other players, eliminating the possibility of theft. I recommend that anybody who tries team play should work out an arrangement like this where no one, not even a spouse or close friend, can handle anyone's money but his or her own.

Sitting Out

One factor hardly ever featured in computer simulations is that it is perfectly acceptable to sit out a few hands in certain circumstances, and this may lessen rather than increase heat. Murmuring "I'll wait until somebody wins a hand" after a series of losses, makes you look like a hunch gambler, and saves you money in a negative count, without the loss of playing time that Wonging involves.

Entering Mid Shoe

If you enter a game already in progress and you have not seen the previous cards then you should assume a count of 0. Many students of the game become confused by this. They think that if they sit down when half of the pack has been dealt and small cards start coming out, that high cards must have come out previously. This is fallacious. The count depends on knowledge of *seen* cards. The fact that a card has been dealt is of no importance. Entering when half the pack has been dealt is equivalent to counting at the start of the shoe; the only difference being that you will see half as many cards before the shuffle.

Number of Hands Per Hour

It is universally the case that blackjack theorists prefer to argue the merits of complicated technical questions concerning the finer points of play, which will not significantly affect the counter's expectation over a lifetime of play, rather than the tactics which genuinely get you more money. There's a simple reason for this; the methods you can really use to win more are often very boring.

Primary among the ways to increase your edge is find a way to obtain a larger bet spread without attracting heat. Another way is simply to play more hands per hour. Most blackjack studies assume a benchmark of 100 hands per hour. This is really for convenience. At a full table you will probably get many fewer hands than this, perhaps as few as thirty. At a heads-up game with a highly-skilled dealer the professional can get in as many as 700 hands per hour. Obviously, the more hands you play, the more money you win. It's an amazing fact that nobody ever mentions—learning how to play fast against quick dealers does more for your win rate than anything. In a heads-up game a dealer will match his/her speed to your own play. You should make a habit of having your next bet ready before the previous hand is finished, there should be no hesitation on your part.

Of course, there is always a trade-off between speed and accuracy of play, and also fatigue. However, there are ways to improve things without imposing a greater strain on your brain. The first is obviously to play games with as few other players as possible. Any more than three, walk away. Often this means you will have to play during the small hours. All other things being equal, do not select a dealer who is slower than your mental processes. One often overlooked factor is time spent shuffling. Professionals rarely consider the loss in expectation due to shuffle time, but casinos do, so learn from them. If they are not shuffle tracking, counters often neglect the importance of the shuffle. If it is a complicated multi-pass shuffle with several riffles then you will be losing several hands in the hour over a casino which uses an automated shuffler. This is more important than the use of a higher-level count, memorizing 150 indices or keeping track of the Aces.

Something never mentioned by other blackjack texts (because it is obvious) is that it is much better to play 150 hands in an hour and make a few mistakes than play 50 hands an hour and play perfectly.

End Play

While the Hi-Lo and other commercial blackjack systems are designed to make the best use of information on how to play your hands, for each individual playing decision the effects of removal are different. The Hi-Lo is very poor at making some decisions, as we have seen, it is of no use at all in telling you whether to hit 14 vs. 10 because it contains no information about the availability of the 7s. However, sometimes it is possible to improvise and make use of information about the other cards on the table during the round.

Take for example a round after the cut card has come out, when you are dealt 14 vs. the dealer's 10. You can forget the Hi-Lo, it is of no use in making this decision.

Cheating the House

I don't cheat, never have, and *don't advise* anyone else to. It's simply not the way I fight. The risks are huge as well.

The dangers involved in the kind of sting operation necessary to make serious money out of a large casino are immense. If you get caught, and you probably will, then at best you can expect prison. At worst, well, a cheat leaves his civil rights at the door.

It is not even financially desirable to cheat. Cheats become so enamored with sleight-of-hand that they never learn how to exploit their legal advantages fully. Sure, if you mark Aces with daub you might have an advantage of 12–13 percent on each and every hand, much more than a card counter. But you might find that you can play very little (overexposure is a much greater danger to a cheat than a card counter) and can only play for stakes of a certain size. To do otherwise is to risk virtually certain detection. The bottom line is that the best counters make more money than the most proficient cheats. The sub-standard counters may break even or lose a little for their efforts but the slightly less proficient cheaters end up in jail. Do you want to be one of those terminal losers who insists on making a dishonest quarter rather than an honest dollar?

One last thing, and in a way this is the most important and valuable passage in the book. If you pursue professional blackjack, sooner or later, somebody will come along and make you a proposition. They will flatter your intellect and try to involve you in a scam. They will make you believe you can make a lot of money with minimal effort. When this situation arises remember, and let these words burn through your brain like Polish vodka, you are the mark.

Hole Card Play

Prior to the publication of this book the main form of play used to get an edge at the tables other than card counting involved knowledge of the dealers hole card.

Amazingly, in the pre-war years, the casinos believed they still had the edge even when *both* dealer cards were exposed. A casino in Winemucca dealt an otherwise ordinary game of single-deck blackjack with a $10 limit, in the 1930s and 40s in just this way—face up! This is something of a testament to the general awfulness of play in the pre-war years. The advantage from perfect knowledge of the hole card is almost 10 percent.

The oldest recorded method of hole card play is known as the "tell." Skilled players can infer something from the body language of a dealer when they peek under a 10 or Ace to see if they have a blackjack in a single-deck game, which is done to save time. Perfect tell play gives you a 2.3 percent advantage over the house.

Another method, credited to Stanford Wong, depends on the aging of the deck structure. The method involves identifying the hole card from its *warp*, which can be distinguishable owing to the practice of checking for a blackjack.

These methods are not currently tenable in the vast majority of casinos in the world, because they depend upon the dealer checking under a 10 for a blackjack, which very few casinos now do. If you do find such a game, then Wong's excellent *Basic Blackjack* (Pi Yee Press) is the definitive work on the subject.

Card Readers

The casinos have in the past few years begun to use devices which automatically check the hole card. Having a dealer check his hole card when he has an Ace or 10 upcard saves time, and therefore makes more money for the casino. But it also renders the casino vulnerable to various advantage-play techniques mentioned in this chapter. It also allows a crooked dealer to tip a confederate player off about the hole card's value. The automatic readers save time and prevent any use of traditional hole-card methods used by professionals.

Auto-peekers are not just mirrors. They check the hole card using an electronic eye and will light up if the eye sees an Ace. The dealer knows no more about the value of the card than the players do. Some of the auto-peekers are only designed to check the card when a 10 is up. When an Ace is up the dealer will check himself as dealers always used to. The dealer may "tell" the value of the hole card in this case, but such opportunities are infrequent and do not provide very clear or useful information.

Specially manufactured cards must be used with card readers (you will notice the index on the Ace is printed twice). Occasionally a casino tries to use a different stock of cards with the reader which often causes Aces and 10s to jam in the machine. This is exploitable information.

Some players believe that the new card reader devices warp the cards, in a manner similar to traditional warps. However, low cards would tend to be "humped" while Aces and 10s would tend to be "cupped." The jury is still out; the hypothesis is plausible, and the sparse figures collated on the subject indicate some effects are in evidence but no statistically significant data has yet been provided from which the player can realize a worthwhile advantage.

Spooking

Spooking is a legally gray technique whereby an agent is stationed behind the dealer to catch a glimpse of the dealer's hole card. It has been immortalized in the film *Casino*. The agent conveys the value of the hole card to a confederate at the table with a prearranged signal. The player then alters his strategy accordingly. Anyone who has seen *Casino* knows the potential dangers of this strategy. (Actually no casino would try that sort of thing now, but you may well end up in jail.)

The gain from spooking is a mere third of that available from front loading. Even if you do not care about cheating it is silly to use a illegal technique which is inferior to some completely legal methods.

Front Loading

Some dealers in hand-held games, perhaps only one in 100, have the unconscious habit of raising the hole card too high as they slip it under their top card. Such dealers are known as *front loaders* and they are money in the bank. With a 100 percent front loader, i.e., a dealer who exposes the value of every card, the maximum possible edge is the 10 percent obtainable from hole card play.

Indexing

Indexing is a term used to describe a method whereby the player can see the value of a card while it is being removed from the top of the deck. A dealer who holds a card up at chest level and pushes the top card over before inserting it in the hole may expose the index corner. The potential edge is the same as with a front-loading player.

Glims

Finally there is the use of a technique known as the *glim*. The *glim* is a term usually applied to a reflective device strategically placed to reveal the dealer's hole card. The deliberate use of such a device is cheating and is not recommended. However, there are sometimes situations where glims can occur naturally. For example, in Frank Scoblete's *Best Blackjack* (Bonus Books) he explains how a stack of shiny dollar chips in the dealer's tray allowed him clear visibility of the hole card.

Nor are glims only useful for learning the value of the dealers hole card. Bryce Carlson in *Blackjack for Blood* explains how the discard tray can reflect the value of the burn card.

Occasionally in a brightly-lit casino I have been able to get a glimpse of the hole card in the reflection of the top of the pack. This requires you to sit in exactly the right position at exactly the right angle for the reflection to be visible. This requires a trained eye. If you practice distinguishing hole cards by subtleties of glare in reflective materials you will learn how to distinguish white space (usually low value) from cards with paint (high value). Polaroid glasses can help you distinguish between cards by eliminating randomly dispersed light.

To take advantage of knowledge of the dealer's hole card you need to know what to do with the information. The hole card basic strategy is presented below.

Hole Card Strategy

Dealer's Hand (Hard)	Hit until (Hard)	(Soft)	Double	Split
20	20	20		
19	19	19	9	
18	18	18	2, 3, 7, 8, 9	
17	17	18	2, 3, 6, 7, 8	
12	12	18	5, 6, 7, 8, 9, 10, 11, A2-A9	all
11	15	18		Ace

Dealer's Hand (Hard)	Hit until (Hard)	(Soft)	Double	Split
10	16	18	11	Ace
9	17	18	10, 11	Ace, 8, 9
8	17	18	10, 11	Ace, 7, 8, 9
7	17	18	10, 11	Ace, 2, 3, 7, 8
6	12	18	9, 10, 11	Ace, 2, 3, 6-9
5	13	18	10, 11, A2-A8	Ace, 2, 3, 6-9
4	14	18	10, 11, A6, A7	Ace, 7, 8
Ace-9	20	20		
Ace-8	19	19		9
Ace-7	18	18		2, 3, 7, 8, 9
Ace-6	17	18		Ace, 2, 3, 6-8
Ace-5	13	18	9, 10, 11	Ace, 2, 3, 6-9
				Ace-6, Ace-7
Ace-4	13	18	10, 11	Ace, 2, 6-9
Ace-3	14	18	10, 11	Ace, 7, 8
Ace-2	15	18	10, 11	Ace, 7, 8
Ace-Ace	16	18	11	Ace, 8

Card Forcing

Another legally gray area is a technique whereby a player gets hold of the cut card and repeatedly stabs it into the deck and twists to see the denomination of the card at the point the deck is opened. If he finds an Ace or a 10 he will remove the cut card and draw it back a centimeter so as to be dealt this card on his first hand. He then bets the table maximum. A player has to do this only once a day to become very wealthy.

Seeing the Top Card

On rare occasions you will find a dealer who tilts the deck and slides the next card forward ready for dealing. You may get a glimpse of this card. A similar thing can happen in shoe games. A bad dealer will slide a card forward ready for dealing out of the lip of the shoe, and then retract it when he realizes they do not need another card as the round has been completed. Again if you are observant you may get a glimpse of this card.

Lastly some jurisdictions (Britain and Atlantic City, for example) require a card exposed in error to be dealt as the first card of the next round. This often happens with dealer totals with multiple cards. Count these totals carefully, especially if you are sitting at first base.

Multicolored Card Backs

Some casinos use a pack with decks of different colored backs. This is to prevent "card-mucking," an illegal sleight-of-hand techniques whereby cards are "switched" from a location secreted on the player's person to the table. It is quite an effective countermeasure against a cheating player, but it can also help the advantage player.

If you can see the color of the top card before it is dealt you can keep a separate count for each color of deck. Say the different decks have red and blue backs. He will count +1 for red cards valued 2–6 and -1 for red Aces or 10s, and he will count -1 for blue cards valued 2–6 and +1 for black Aces and 10s. This can work beautifully in team play as the Small Player knows at all times which type of cards are more likely to be low and which are high. He plays his hands in order to give the Big Player the type of card he needs.

For example, if the Big Player needs a small card, and the Small Player knows that there is an excess of small cards in the red portion of the pack, and an excess of high cards in the blue portion of the pack, and that a red card is waiting in the shoe, then he will not take the card. This may mean the Small Player does not take a hit when basic strategy says he should. This will allow the Big Player to take a card which is more likely to help his hand.

If the Small Player took the red card, the Big Player would have to take a card which might have a blue or red back and would on average be less likely to be small. Conversely the Small Player would hit his hand if the next card is likely to be high, or stand if the Big Player required a high card, and so on.

Chapter 15
The Stacker Play

One of the most powerful and until now, one the greatest secrets of advantage play, is called the *stacker play*. It is a highly advanced team technique again taught to me by the mysterious Englishman known as the *Green Baize Vampire*. The Vampire described the technique to me as it was carried out during one of his team's most successful coups.

Whilst in Hungary we scouted for a hand-held game with an easy shuffle. We found a two-deck game where the dealer just used two riffles on each deck segment. One of the girls, Cathy, would play heads-up against the dealer. She'd be betting five dollars, the table minimum, on three hands. She'd stand on virtually everything. This looks crazy, but the pit wrote her off as another stupid female player. But there was a method to the madness. She would send the cards back to the dealer in high-low, high-low order. She did it like the house does, face down, real smooth. They never suspected her. She never took any hit cards so she could control as many cards as possible.

By the end of the deck about 60 percent of the cards were in the predetermined sequence we'd created. The shuffle changes the order, but it leaves the cards in sequence. If a high card comes out you know the card after the next one will be low and vice versa. The cards were in an order that naturally favors the players, mainly because blackjacks are more frequent. More important we had a pretty accurate prediction for over half the cards in the deck.

Two players hit the felt. Cathy was sitting at first base. A Big player bet $1,000 a hand in the center of the table, while another girl, Lucy, pretended to be the high roller's girlfriend and bet five dollars in third base. Cathy would take either one or two hands so that the BP got a high card while Lucy would ensure that the dealer got a low card. Moreover they would both play their hands so that the BP received a high or low hit card and conversely the dealer got a card which sent him stiff or bust. Lucy and Cathy lost most of their chips, since they were deviating heavily from basic strategy. But the high roller (also a skilled sequence tracker and card counter) won $20,000 wiping out their losses many times over. It was clinical, precise, devastating.

The Vampire is talking about a game with a very high level of prediction of each actual card (over 80 percent). This is a best-case scenario, and it should be remembered that sequence tracking alone would yield spectacular rewards in such a game.

Stacking is a very advanced team technique that should not even be attempted by most professional players. It requires several players, iron nerve, and a great Act, to operate successfully. Nonetheless, it can be spectacularly profitable. Like sequencing, its effectiveness can be easily demonstrated.

Deal out a deck of cards, one at a time, placing each card on top of the last one in a new stack. Now deal them out again in the exact same order, this time playing hands of blackjack against yourself, seeing if you can predict the value of each card. Most people will have great difficulty remembering the order of half a dozen or more cards. Now deal out the cards again only this time make two stacks, one for 10s and Aces, one for all other cards. The Aces and 10s stack will be shorter than the other so take some cards off the small card stack till it is approximately the same height as the high card stack.

Then play hands of blackjack, only this time take cards alternately from each stack. Try and make intelligent use of the fact that you know each card is high or low. You will see that you can win more with much less strain on the memory.

Now, in a real game of blackjack, the dealer will shuffle, which destroys some, but not all, of our prediction. For example, if initially adjacent cards remain together 10 percent of the time, and the cards are in high-low, high-low order, then whenever you see a high card you will know a low card will follow with greater frequency than the pure odds would suggest.

This method requires a hand-held game to operate successfully. The player is usually allowed to send back his first two cards in whatever order he chooses. If the player is not allowed the option to return the cards in the order of his or her choosing the method is not effective (some sequences could be created with selective splitting, however this could only be used to influence a relatively small number of cards at great cost).

Because the player has no control over how his hit cards are ordered it is better for a Small Player to stand whenever possible (heat allowing). This carries a high toll, the player who stands on everything above 11 loses at the rate of 9.5 percent faster than basic strategy. If you are using this method as a solo player, do not deviate from basic strategy. However, for well-financed teams, the greater control over the cards is justified if the Small Player's table minimum bets are much smaller than the Big Player's. The beauty of stacking is that, unlike sequence tracking, no memorization is required. The Big Player knows the (rough) order of each and every card without having been present at the table.

How much gain can we obtain from stacking? You can get a rough estimate with the following figures: if you knew you were going to get a high card, either a 10 or an Ace (9s and 8s don't count for this purpose because a 9 does not give us any advantage as a first card) you would have an advantage of 21 percent. Similarly if you knew the dealer was going to get a low card you would have a 13 percent edge. A total of 34 percent edge on each and every hand is pretty good, but we are not talking about perfect prediction of course, just a subtle shifting of percentages.

Not all the cards can be ordered in high-low sequence, and those that are may be stripped or cut away by the shuffle, so our edge is unlikely to be more than a twentieth of this figure. If the shuffle is such that we can arrange things so that the dealer can get the low card and we get the high card more than 20 percent of the time than the we will have a 3.4 percent edge. Of course we can probably only order about half the cards owing to the number of cutoff and dealer cards, which we cannot control, so our edge is roughly half that. Further we will have a pretty good idea what the dealer hole card is, since we get to see what the card before and the card after the hole card is. Our prediction is much more accurate than when we predict the next card.

Firstly, if you knew with 100 percent certainty whether the hole card was high or low you would have a 3.5 percent edge. Unfortunately, we do not have quite that much accuracy. However, according to Stanford Wong's *Basic Blackjack* (Pi Yee Press), if we have a 46 percent chance of being accurate when predicting 10s and Aces and 71 percent accuracy when predicting 2s through 9s, then just by knowing when to take insurance, not doubling 11 vs. 10, doubling 10 vs. 10, then you get 0.83 percent over basic strategy.

You can also gain from making play departures from basic strategy based on your prediction of whether your hit card will be high or low. Don't overdo this, restrict it to situations where your count is right on the number for changing strategy, as in this case it can't hurt to use the knowledge from stacking. Resist the temptation to make ill-advised strategy changes which contradict the count.

Chapter 16

Internet Casinos and Cyberspace Blackjack

Recently there has been much interest in the creation of a new industry of "online" casinos, virtual gaming parlors you can visit without leaving your home which exist only in cyberspace on your computer screen. For a long time there have been computer programs created for you to play your favorite casino games, including blackjack, but the difference is that you can now play for real money via the Internet.

When I first wrote about Internet casinos in my book *Baccarat for the Clueless* (Carol Publishing) I was very guarded about the new technology. To summarize my misgivings: it is simply far too easy for the online casinos to cheat. A program can easily be written to appear to offer a fair game of blackjack, yet actually favor the house so the player loses far more per hand than in the real casino game. If you are cheated there is no way to prove it and nothing you can do about it even if you could. The casinos are often based in a country chosen for its lack of effective legislation and/or enforcement against gambling fraud.

I have revised this opinion.

Not because the cyberspace casino industry has proven itself honest. It manifestly has not, and currently the effects at self-policing are a joke. Numerous examples exist of netcasinos refusing to pay up, ignoring all attempts at communication and disappearing. Moreover many casinos in existence offer games which are blatantly fixed as I described above. Yet, many offer games that are accurate representations of the odds as they would be in the real world, and a handful have established a tentative credibility. But still fraud is a very serious problem.

No, the reason I changed my mind is that I learned how an intelligent player may be able to play with an advantage against the netcasinos. The new industry is currently one of the fastest growing elements of the Internet. Literally billions of dollars are at stake, competition is fierce, and cyberspace is already congested with outfits vying for supremacy. To obtain their share of the market the fledgling organizations use very aggressive tactics. Almost all offer incentives of some kind, which are comparable and sometimes exceed the complimentaries offered by real casinos. Generally this is an award for $20 or $25, but it may be far more exotic, and is only limited by the imagination of the owners.

The money is a reward for signing up and making a first bet or for a certain amount of "action" (total sum of money bet). If the game has reasonable rules and the game is not rigged, the skilled player will usually be able to play enough to satisfy the requirements for the bonus and make a small total profit. At the time of this writing, there are hundreds of such casinos in existence, so a shrewd player can do this systematically and profit continuously. And there is indeed a new class of professional gambler emerging called the *net matchplay hustler*.

For example, say you find a netcasino with a house edge of 0.5 percent using basic strategy, and a $25 bonus for joining. You play 300 hands betting five dollars. Your expected loss is $7.50, giving you $17.50 profit. Not a spectacular amount, but if you can do it often enough, a tidy extra income.

It is often pointed out by new players that you can join a cyberspace casino and use another computer to calculate the optimal blackjack strategy on each and every hand. Interesting as this sounds, it is not easy or practical for a number of reasons.

Firstly, the majority of netcasinos shuffle up after every hand. So, counting cannot really be used. In single-deck games memorizing all the exceptions to basic strategy when you take into consideration your first two cards and not just their total will give you about 0.04 percent over basic strategy, and virtually nothing in multiple deck. This will probably not be factored into any calculations the netcasino makes about your loss rate. The two-card basic strategy is explained in Appendix C.

There are more exceptions to basic strategy when you take into consideration three or more cards. One easy to remember and valuable rule is, stand on 16 vs 10 with three or more cards that do not contain a 6. To achieve a higher expectation, things get more complex. No specialist commercial software exists to take you further, you have to write it yourself, which is no mean feat.

You can improve further on your basic-strategy expectation by using the best linear estimates of removal for the most important plays. This can be worked out with pen and paper without the use of another computer. Here are the most important:

	A	2	3	4	5	6	7	8	9	10	Mean
Insurance	1.81	1.81	1.81	1.81	1.81	1.81	1.81	1.81	1.81	-4.07	-7.69
16 vs. 10	-0.49	-0.29	-.80	-1.73	-2.57	1.65	-0.71	-0.06	0.55	1.12	-0.45
15 vs. 10	-0.17	0.19	-0.32	-0.73	-1.75	-2.23	-0.54	0.09	0.66	1.20	3.11
14 vs. 10	-0.08	0.44	0.17	-0.26	-0.77	-1.41	-4.21	0.22	0.77	1.28	6.64

As an example, if you had 14 vs. 10, and your hand was made up of two 7s, subtract 4.21 x 2 = 8.24. Then subtract from 6.64, the figure on the far right, which is the off-the-top advantage for favorability for hitting over standing. In this case you get -1.6. The minus sign tells you that standing is now better than hitting The list of figures for every single possible play is contained in Peter Griffin's *Theory of Blackjack*. It is very lengthy and cannot be reproduced here.

A further possibility for profit exists in joining a casino "affiliate" program. On the Internet "affiliate" refers to the owner of a website who creates a link to the netcasino, i.e. someone who advertises a netcasino. The affiliate receives a percentage of the profits from anyone joining the netcasino through his advertisement. The scheme is attractive to advertisers because the profits are potentially limitless. It is attractive to the netcasino because there is no risk, they only pay out a part of what the advertiser brings in.

In theory at least some netcasinos frown on affiliates joining the netcasino via their own advertisement. But it is impossible to prevent in practice, particularly with a partner or syndicate. Naturally, an affiliate who joins the netcasino he is connected with effectively gets reimbursed part of his loss, similar to the "cashback" programs operated by real-world casinos. Because the affiliate returns can be quite high, 25–40 percent, this is quite important.

When you sign up to an affiliate program (the netcasino will usually explain how to do this with a clear series of step by step instructions) you fill out a form giving your details and the netcasino will send you an e-mail containing an Internet address. It will look something like this: http://www.williamhillcasino.com/index.php3?501416.

The idea is that you put this address in an advertisement for the casino on your own webpage, but it is not essential to do this if you just want to take advantage of the affiliate scheme yourself. In fact, you do not even need your own webpage, or need to know anything about programming. Just type the address in straight away and you will find yourself at the netcasino. If you now sign up as a customer you will find you start earning affiliate commissions.

Of course, many of the seasoned players who mock those who join netcasinos as "lambs to the slaughter" are quite incapable of detecting the clumsiest dealing of a second

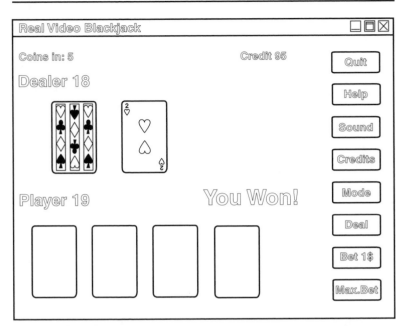

A typical screen layout for an Internet blackjack game

in a real-world casino, let alone the invisible skills of the best card sharps, who are difficult even for another sleight-of-hand expert to spot even when he knows what is happening. Card counting does not enable to you to detect cheating any more than it enables you to deal.

You run a certain amount of risk, so protect yourself as best you can. Let that axiom guide you in virtual and actual play.

To join an Internet casino requires you to have computer access and to provide the casino that you wish to join with your credit card details. It is for this reason that many people are very suspicious of these organizations. Every time you play a game, your account is debited or credited automatically with the amount that you win or lose.

The rules are typically identical to those of ordinary blackjack, and just as varied. As with most of long-distance computer communication, the games are slow and jerky, and considering the level of sophistication that computer graphics have achieved in the last few years.

The cards are "shuffled" much more thoroughly than any human shuffle. This is because the cards are dealt according to pseudo-random numbers. These are a sequence of numbers generated by a Random Number Generator (RNG). The RNG may be either a special electronic circuit or a piece of computer software. The numbers appear completely unconnected with each other but do in fact follow a very complex series. If you could figure this series out you could predict what cards would be dealt and make a lot of money. Unfortunately, this is very difficult to do. You will not find how to do this in any library, it is a very important part of military intelligence (it is connected with code breaking) and writings on the subject are usually kept confidential. Nevertheless, certain netcasinos have gone bankrupt allegedly due to the use of very sloppy RNG's whose patterns were easy for hackers to figure out. This is almost impossible if the software designers are competent.

If you are still interested I can only offer the following advice:

1. Only join an Internet casino that claims to offer blackjack with the same odds as the real casino game, and preferably one which has been independently tested for accuracy. This is by no means a guarantee that the game is honest, but without such an assurance the game is almost certainly dishonest.

2. Most cyberspace casinos will have software that you can download and play without actually having to risk money on it. Play a few hundred hands of blackjack and see if this accords with your experience in the real world. Any serious fixing of the game would probably become apparent. Again, the software you can download and play for free is not necessarily the same as the software you use when playing for actual money, but if the free software does not accord with

your experience of actual blackjack you can bet your life the play-for-money software is rigged too.

3. If you sign up to a casino and play for real stakes, then do keep a careful tally of your wins and losses and the number of hands you have played. If you are unsure whether you are being cheated, take out a statistics textbook and do a Chi-squared or Poisson distribution test on your results, which will give you a good indication. If the idea of setting out to do this fills you with mathematical dread, then you could try posting a question to one of the mathematics or gambling newsgroups on the Internet, and you will probably find that there is someone who is willing and able to perform these calculations for you.

4. Never join an Internet casino which states in its rules and regulations something to the effect of "For personal rather than professional use only." This means "No journalists or other individuals who might expose us for the crooks we are, strictly suckers only." If they have nothing to hide they would not fear investigation. The reputable casinos will invite independent testers to try out their software, in order to verify its fairness.

5. Only buy-in to any such organization for the absolute minimum, at least until you've established you're getting a fair deal.

6. Try and find out other people's experiences with the casino before you join. If you look in the archives at *http://www.dejanews.com*, you may find many uncensored stories about people's dealings with many of the operational casinos.

7. Do not tolerate any delay in payment of winnings you have rightfully won. Do not listen to any excuses or put up with any procrastination from them. There is no reasonable excuse. More likely they are trying to withhold payment for as long as possible in order to accumulate interest on money which has been won legitimately by their clients, if indeed they have any intention of paying you at all.

Finally, the Internet itself has revolutionized the nature of blackjack discussion.

New players can learn from *Rolling Good Times Online*, the internet magazine, which has contributions from some of the best blackjack writers in the field such as Henry Tamburin, John Grochowski, Andy Glazer, Fred Renzey and others (*www.scoblete.com*). Previously card counters existed in isolation or in small secretive groups. The very nature of the profession made any kind of communication difficult. With the rise of Internet it is possible for players to communicate on a daily basis without having to directly reveal their identity.

At the time of writing there are many excellent commercial discussion groups, such as Arnold Snyder's *www.rge21.com*, Michael Dalton's *www.bjrnet.com*, and Stanford Wong's *www.bj21.com*. There are also non-commercial organizations such as *Rec.Gambling.Blackjack-Moderated*. Lastly there is my own forum, the Card counters Cafe at *http://clubs.yahoo.com/clubs/blackjackcardcounterscafe*.

Membership is free and all are welcome regardless of their level of play. Remember, the only stupid questions are the ones you do not ask!

Appendix A
Glossary

Back Counting: Card counting without actually sitting at the table and playing.

Bankroll: The set amount of money you have to play with. This does not include money for living expenses or other essentials.

Bust: When a player's or dealer's total exceeds 21 they are said to have "bust."

Card Counting: A method designed to detect and exploit favorable situations in blackjack by observing the dealt cards and hence keeping track of the undealt cards.

Cut Card: A plain plastic card provided for the player who, at the invitation of the dealer, inserts it into a stack of cards after they have been shuffled.

Deal: The distribution of the cards.

Deck: 52 cards: four Aces, four cards each value 2 through 10, and four jacks, kings, and queens.

Discards: Cards that are set aside from play having been dealt, not to reappear until after the shuffle.

Kelly Betting: Betting the percentage of your bankroll according to the percent advantage you enjoy, divided by the ratio of a winning wager to a losing wager.

Hand: Any two cards dealt to the player or the dealer, together with any subsequent cards they may take.

Hard Total: Any total not containing an Ace.

Hole Card: The card taken as one of the first two dealer cards, placed face down.

House Edge: The percentage, on average, of money placed as bets which will be gained by the casino.

Insurance: A sidebet available when the dealer has an Ace. If the dealer has a ten you win 2-1 on your insurance bet, otherwise the insurance bet is lost.

Natural: If the player's or dealer's first two cards consist of a 10 and an Ace the hand is called a "natural" or "blackjack." The player is paid 3-2 on a blackjack while the player only loses his original bet if the dealer is dealt a natural.

Packs: The name for any number of 52-card decks mixed together in a game of blackjack.

Penetration: The number of cards dealt out of the pack, typically expressed as a percentage.

Preferential Shuffle: The act of shuffling the cards whenever their composition is favorable to the player.

Push: A tie between player and dealer.

Riffle: Taking two groups of cards and interweaving one into the other.

Round: A round refers to the dealing of each player and dealer hand and the settling of the hand with the appropriate payoffs.

Running Count: The running total of the card-count values of the dealt cards.

Sequencing: A method designed to exploit the riffling action of the dealer by noting adjacent cards and the knowledge that they are likely to remain in close proximity after the shuffle.

Shoe: The box into which multiple decks of cards are placed after being shuffled and cut, and from which they are taken during the game.

Soft Total: A hand containing one or more Aces.

Shuffle: The complete procedure used by the dealer for reordering the cards.

Stripping: This is when the dealer takes a segment of cards with one hand and takes cards from the top with the other hand onto the table, reversing the card order.

Third Base: The last seat on the dealer's right.

True Count: The running total of the card-count values divided by the number of decks remaining.

Unbalanced Count: A count system in which the point count values do not sum to zero.

Upcard: The card which is taken as one of the first two dealer cards which is dealt face up.

Appendix B
Bibliography

Baldwin, Roger R.; Cantey, Wilbert E.; Maisel, Herbert; and Mcdermott, James P. *The Optimum Strategy in Blackjack.* Journal of the American Statistical Association September, 1956.

Black, Jacques. *The Money-Spinners.* Herpenden, Herts, UK: Oldcastle Books, 1998.

Canfield, Robert Albert. *Blackjack Your Way to Riches!* New Jersey: Lyle Stuart. Inc., 1979.

Carlson, Bryce. *Blackjack for Blood.* California: CompuStar Press, 1997.

Epstein, Richard A. *The Theory of Gambling and Statistical Logic.* New York: Academic Press, 1967.

Griffin, Peter A. *The Theory of Blackjack.* LasVegas: Huntington Press, 1996.

Humble, Lance. Ph.D. and Cooper, Carl, Ph.D. *The World's Greatest Blackjack Book.* New York: Doubleday & Co., 1980.

Malmuth, Mason. *Gambling Theory and Other Topics*. Las Vegas: 2+2 Publishing, 1994.

Marshall, Angie. *A Woman's Guide to Blackjack*. New Jersey: Carol Publishing, 1999.

May, John. *Baccarat for the Clueless*. New Jersey: Carol Publishing, 1998.

Revere, Lawrence. *Playing Blackjack as a Business*. Las Vegas: Paul Mann Publishing Co., 1973.

Scoblete, Frank. *Best Blackjack*. Chicago: Bonus Books, 1996.

Sklansky, David. *Getting the Best Of It*. Las Vegas: 2+2 Publishing, 1997.

Snyder, Arnold. *Blackbelt in Blackjack*. Oakland: RGE Publishing, 1981.

Thorp, Edward O., Ph.D. *Beat the Dealer*. 2nd Edition. New York: Vintage Books, 1966.

Thorp, Edward O., Ph. D. *The Mathematics of Gambling*. Hollywood: Gambling Times Incorporated, 1984.

Uston, Kenneth. *Million Dollar Blackjack*. Hollywood: Gambling Times Incorporated, 1981.

Vancura, Olaf, Ph. D. *Smart Casino Gambling*. California: Index Publishing Group, Inc., 1996.

Roberts, Stanley, Editor. *The Gambling Times Guide to Blackjack*. New Jersey: Carol Publishing, 1994.

Wong, Stanford. *Basic Blackjack*. La Jolla: Pi Yee Press, 1995.

———. *Professional Blackjack*. La Jolla: Pi Yee Press, 1994.

Appendix C
Basic Strategy for Single Deck

Hard Hands

When to draw:	When to split:	When to double:
	Split 2s, 3s & 7s vs. 2-7	Double-down 9 vs. 2-6
	Split 6s vs. 2-6	Double-down 10 vs. 2-9
Draw to 11 vs. all	Split 8s vs. 2-9	Double-down 11 vs. all
Draw to 12 vs. 2 or 3	Split 9s 2-9 except 7	Double-down 13-16 vs. 4, 5, 6
Draw to 16 vs. 7-10	Split Aces vs. all except Aces	Double-down 17 vs. 2, 3, 4, 5, 7
Draw to 16 vs. Ace		Double-down 18 vs. 3, 4, 5, 6
		Double-down 19 vs. 6

Soft hands

Draw to Ace-6 vs. all (including Aces)

Draw to Ace-7 vs. 9-10

If the dealer hits soft 17, then hit soft 18 against A and stand with T, 2 vs. 6 and T, 3 vs. 2*

Double 6, 2 vs. 5**

If double after split is permitted split 2-2 vs. 2, 3, 3 vs. 2, 3, 8, 4-4 vs. 4-6, 6-6 vs. 7

7-7 vs. 8, 9-9 vs. A if dealer hits soft 17

* Great credit for this discovery, which was also not contained in Peter Griffin's calculations, must go to Gustav Shoe, a former reporter for *Blackjack Forum*

** Credit must go to Steve Jacobs, the pioneer of the *Internet rec.gambling* newsgroup for this discovery

Index

About the Frank Scoblete Get-the-Edge Guides

Gaming's number one writer, Frank Scoblete, has signed some of the top new talent in the gaming world to join him in producing a line of books that will give the advantage to the player at games where this is theoretically possible such as Blackjack, Poker, and Video Poker *and* at games where it is "practically" possible such as Roulette and Craps. When it is not theoretically or practically possible to get a real edge, the **Frank Scoblete Get-the-Edge Guides** will do the next best thing—give you strategies that can reduce the house edge to the minimum and increase the casino comps to the maximum.

Now available: *Thrifty Gambling: More Casino Fun for Less Risk!* by John G. Brokopp.

Look for the following Frank Scoblete Get-the-Edge Guides in the near future: *Get the Edge at Craps: How to Become a Rhythmic Roller!* by The Sharpshooter; *Get the Edge at Roulette: How to Predict Where the Ball Will Land!* by Christopher Pawlicki; *Get the Edge at Video Poker: Simple, Powerful Strategies for the Recreational Player!* by John Robison.

The New Chance and Circumstance Magazine

Subscribe to Frank Scoblete's quarterly magazine, *The New Chance and Circumstance*, featuring today's hottest writers writing about all aspects of casino play. Join Frank Scoblete, John Grochowski, Walter Thomason, John May, John Robison, Chris Pawlicki, Henry Tamburin, Alene Paone, Catherine Poe, The Sharpshooter, Barney Vinson, The Bootlegger and many more in each and every issue. Call 1-800-944-0406 or write to: Paone Press, Box 610, Lynbrook, NY 11563.

Zender, Bill. *Card-Counting for the Casino Executive*. Las Vegas, 1990.